AUSTRALIA WIDE COOKBOOK

Photography by
KEN DUNCAN

Recipes by
VALWYN McMONIGAL

INTRODUCTION

Australia! The largest island in the world and certainly the most spectacular. We are blessed with a wonderful variety of scenery and culture and a marvellous array of food.

The Australian style of cuisine had humble beginnings, from the roasted witchetty grubs favoured by the Aboriginal people to the meagre, indigestible rations of the first English settlers. The gold rushes of the 19th century attracted many Chinese migrants who brought exotic foods, vegetables and spices. More recently, the post-war migration of many people from Southern Europe, especially Italy, has given us marvellous pasta dishes, sauces and a taste for fresh herbs. All these influences have resulted in a unique cuisine which is a mouthwatering blend of all that is best in Eastern and Western food.

The *Australia Wide Cookbook* will take you on a lavish gastronomic tour of this wonderful land of contrasts. Travel to a tropical paradise and indulge in the delicious fresh seafood, then go to the barren yet beautiful Outback to sample native berries and other 'bush tucker'. We will take you through gentle pastures where the wheat grows and the cattle graze, and then up over mountain ranges, where you'll stop at a breathtaking gorge for a barbecue.

Wherever you go in the *Australia Wide Cookbook*, you will sample foods that are as vibrant and unique as the scenery before you. Come—travel with us! See this wonderful country and sample the cuisine that is truly Australian.

Front Cover: *Timeless Land, Uluru, NT.*
Left: *Erskine Falls, VIC.*

CONTENTS

Sunrise, Uluru, N.T.

VICTORIA

Roast lamb dinner with mint sauce **8**

Cauliflower cheese **9**

Bread roll stuffed with chicken pâté **10**

Blueberry pie with thick lavender cream **11**

Stuffed pork ribs with cherry sauce **12**

Peach Melba **13**

NEW SOUTH WALES

Sydney rock oysters **16**

Carnival of stir fry vegetables with linguini **17**

Wattleseed ice-cream with macadamia tuiles **18**

Yabbies in green coats **20**

Lamb in macadamia crust with mango jus **21**

Bananas in chocolate mud **22**

Powder puffs **23**

TASMANIA

Potato soup with garlic croutons **26**

Tasmanian trout with almonds **27**

Cradle Mountain apple **28**

Scallops with cheesy topping **29**

Smoked salmon wrapped in a potato crepe **32**

Crayfish freshly grilled with lemon butter **33**

Mussels swimming in garlic and brandy **34**

Apple and caraway seed bread **35**

SOUTH AUSTRALIA

Kangaroo'n beer **38**

Pear with fresh fig custard **39**

Quail, olives and sun-dried tomato **40**

Fresh asparagus dressed with walnut **41**

Aussie meat pie **42**

Fruit crumble with whipped cream **44**

Boiled fruit cake **45**

WESTERN AUSTRALIA

Prawns in quandong chilli syrup **48**

Oxtail stew **49**

Dilly bag steak filled with chickpea paste **51**

Whole snapper with tuna mousseline **52**

Our own pavlova **53**

Bread and butter pudding **56**

Anzac biscuits **57**

THE NORTHERN TERRITORY

Eggs in a hole **60**

Damper dripping with golden syrup **60**

Seared buffalo fillet with goat cheese **61**

Barramundi with orange **63**

Crocodile with curry mayonnaise **64**

Black barramundi **66**

Pawpaw mousse wrapped in spun sugar **67**

QUEENSLAND

Chicken kebabs in a peanut coating **70**

Pillows of Moreton Bay bug with relish **71**

Flambe of tropical fruits **73**

Pumpkin scones **74**

Pumpkin soup **74**

Mud crab in coconut sauce **75**

Lamingtons **77**

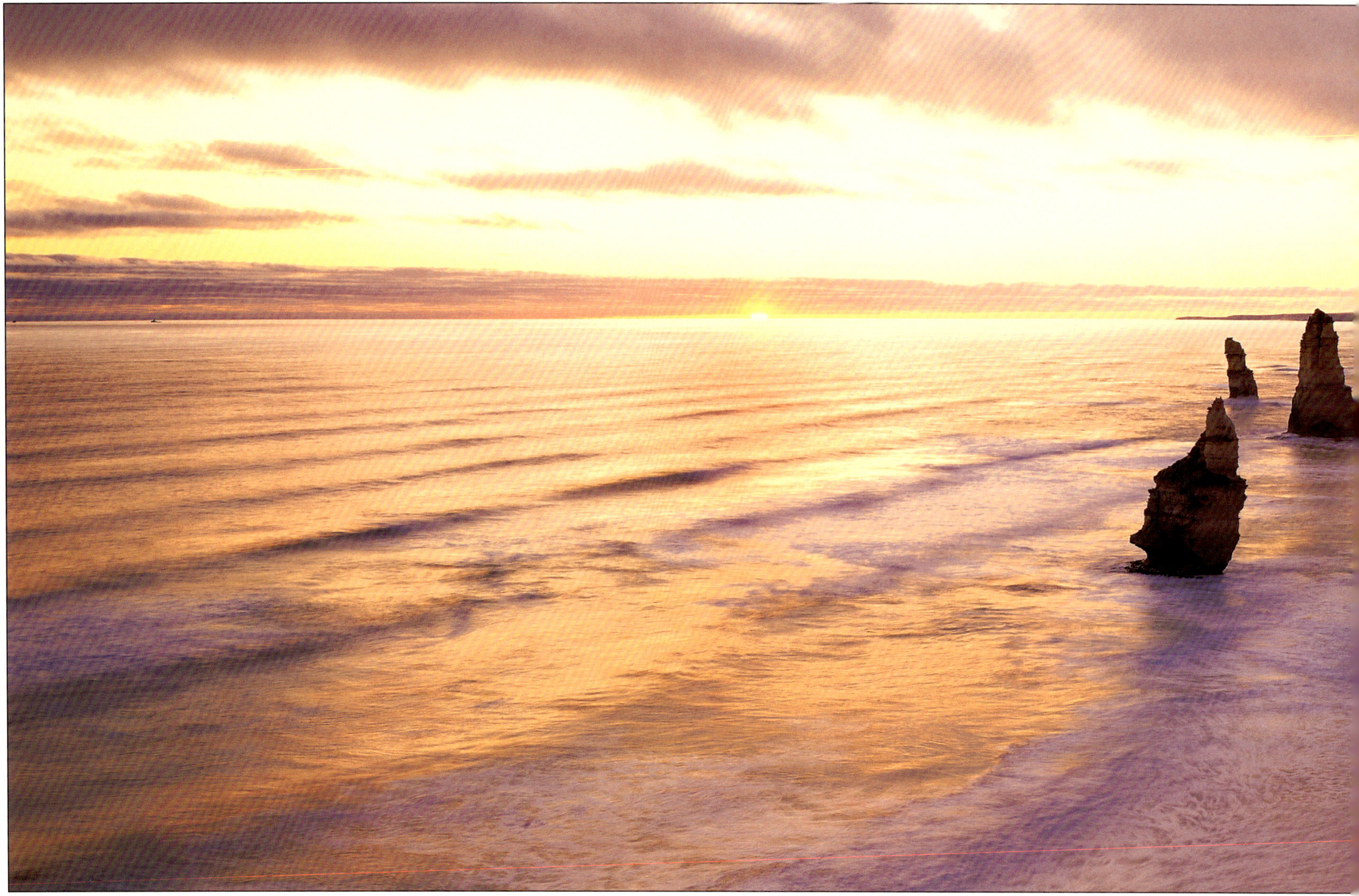

VICTORIA

Drive along the Great Ocean Road, which runs beside the notorious 'Shipwreck Coast'. Take in magnificent views of the Twelve Apostles and visit the charming coastal resorts which are dotted along the way. Then continue over the Otway Ranges, pausing to gaze down the thickly wooded hillsides before going on to the forested cliff tops.

To the north, the dense forests give way to gentle pastoral scenes of wheat, fruit and berry crops, and paddocks where sheep and cattle graze. Often the glint of a tiny church spire can be seen in the small towns which nestle in these soft hills. The sight may bring back memories of returning home after Sunday Service to the tempting aroma of a roast lamb dinner, 'just like Mum used to make'.

Sunrise, Twelve Apostles, VIC.

ROAST LAMB DINNER

1 leg lamb
2 small sprigs each of fresh rosemary, basil and thyme or ½ teaspoon each of the dried herbs
hot water
6 potatoes, peeled
3 sweet potatoes or parsnips, peeled
6 pieces pumpkin, peeled and cut into 5 cm/2 in wedges
6 onions, peeled
12 small yellow squash
500 g/16 oz green peas, shelled

❀ Preheat oven to moderate/180°C/375°F.

❀ Remove skin from lamb. Place lamb on a rack in a baking pan and sprinkle the top with herbs. Pour sufficient hot water into pan to cover base of pan, approximately 2.5 cm/1 in deep. Place in oven to cook, allowing 45 minutes per 1 kg/2 lb cooking time.

❀ Cut potatoes in half, lengthwise. Cut sweet potatoes or parsnips into rounds, approximately 5 cm/2 in thick. Place all vegetables, except squash and peas, in a bowl of cold water for 20 minutes.

❀ One hour before meat is cooked, drain vegetables, retaining some water to cook the peas and squash in. Place the vegetables on the rack around meat. Bake for 30 minutes, turn vegetables, roast a further 15 minutes or until the vegetables are tender and brown.

❀ Cook squash and peas in retained vegetable water, by either boiling, steaming or microwaving until tender.

❀ When meat is cooked and vegetables are tender, remove from rack (meat should still be pink on the inside). Turn oven off. Place vegetables on a plate and return to oven. Cover meat with a cloth and allow to stand while making gravy.

❀ Drain squash and peas, retaining the vegetable water for gravy. Keep squash and peas hot in a covered dish in the oven.

❀ To serve, carve meat thinly and arrange on 6 warmed dinner plates. Arrange baked vegetables, squash and peas around meat slices. Pour a little gravy over the meat. Serve mint sauce in a jug at the table.

❀ This dinner is delicious if served with cauliflower cheese as a side vegetable.

SERVES 6

GRAVY

2 tablespoons plain flour
water from vegetables

❀ Mix flour into the drippings left in the baking pan, stir over heat until flour starts to simmer and brown. Stir in the water from vegetables, return to heat, stir until gravy thickens, adding a little more water if gravy is too thick. Pour into a jug or gravy boat and keep warm in oven.

MINT SAUCE

1 bunch of mint, leaves only
1 teaspoon sugar
2 teaspoons vinegar
3 tablespoons boiling water

❀ Finely chop mint leaves and place in a bowl. Add in sugar, vinegar and boiling water, press leaves into water with a spoon to allow flavour to escape. Pour into a jug. Allow to stand at room temperature.

CAULIFLOWER CHEESE

This is a great favourite, served as a vegetable accompaniment, a complete dish, an entree or as leftovers served on toast for breakfast.

1 small cauliflower
warm salted water
40 g/1½ oz butter
1 tablespoon plain flour
1 cup/250 ml/8 fl oz milk
2 tablespoons grated tasty cheese
chopped parsley, to garnish

❧ Preheat griller or oven to a moderate temperature, about 180°C/375°F.
Break cauliflower into flowerets and soak in warm salted water for 3–4 minutes (this removes any dirt and small insects).

❧ Drain and place in a pan with hot water. Cover and bring to boil, reduce heat and simmer until flowerets are tender. If you prefer to cook in a microwave, place drained flowerets in a dish with 1 tablespoon of hot water and cook on HIGH for 5 minutes then allow to stand for 2 minutes.

❧ While cauliflower is cooking, melt butter in a pan, add flour, stir over heat until flour starts to bubble, remove from heat. Stir in milk, return to heat and stir until mixture boils and thickens.

❧ Remove from heat, add cheese and let it melt into the sauce. To cook sauce in microwave, place butter in a dish, cook on HIGH for 30 seconds, stir in flour and milk, cook on HIGH for 2 minutes, add cheese and beat until smooth.

❧ Drain cooked cauliflower, place on serving plates, spoon cheese sauce over cauliflower and sprinkle with parsley. Alternatively, place cauliflower in a dish, top with cheese sauce, cook under griller or in a hot oven, until sauce browns lightly then sprinkle with parsley.

❧ SERVES 6

Murray River.

Bread Roll Stuffed with Chicken Pâté

This recipe is great as a picnic or supper dish.

500 g/16 oz butter
2 Spanish onions, sliced finely
500 g/16 oz chicken livers, washed
8 garlic cloves, crushed
4 anchovy fillets
1 teaspoon freshly ground pepper
1 French stick of bread or 6 small, round rolls
1 tablespoon oil, extra
1 teaspoon garlic, extra, crushed

❈ Preheat oven to moderate/180°C/375°F.
Melt butter in a frying pan, cook onion and livers until the inside of the livers start to turn pale pink. If you prefer to cook in a microwave, cook butter, onion and livers on HIGH for 5 minutes.

❈ Chop livers roughly and place in a bowl with onions, crushed garlic, anchovies and pepper. Mix well.

❈ Cut one end from bread/rolls, pull out centre leaving a shell 3.5 cm/1½ in thick with dough. Push pâté tightly into the bread cavity and seal with the cut end of bread, securing with toothpicks or skewers.

❈ Mix extra oil and garlic together, brush over top and sides of bread. Bake for 10 minutes. Cool slightly to handle.

❈ To serve, remove both ends of bread. Cut into thick slices. May be eaten warm or cold.

SERVES 6-8

> Anchovies are found in bays and estuaries, mainly south of the Tropic of Capricorn.

Split Point Lighthouse, Airys Inlet.

Blueberry Pie with Thick Lavender Cream

PASTRY

2 cups/250 g/8 oz plain flour

1 tablespoon icing sugar

185 g/6 oz soft butter

squeeze of lemon juice

cold water

extra flour, for rolling

FILLING

430 g/13½ oz blueberries, fresh, canned or frozen

½ cup/125 g/4 oz sugar (not necessary for canned blueberries)

2 eggs, beaten

1 teaspoon cinnamon

2 cups/500 ml/16 fl oz cream

extra 1 cup/250 ml/8 fl oz cream, to serve

2 teaspoons lavender honey, to serve

- Preheat oven to moderate/180°C/375°F.
- Grease an 18 cm/7 in pie plate or 20 cm/8 in quiche pan.
- To prepare the pastry, place flour and sugar in a bowl, rub the butter into the flour with the tips of fingers until it resembles fine breadcrumbs. With a knife, cut the lemon juice and cold water into the flour mixture, adding a little more water, if necessary, until the mixture forms a firm dough. Turn dough out onto a floured sheet and roll pastry to line pie dish. Chill pastry shell while the filling is prepared.
- To prepare the filling, place blueberries into pie base (drain canned berries). Combine all other ingredients and carefully pour over the berries.
- Bake for 30–35 minutes, or until crust is brown and filling is set.
- To serve, whip extra cream and honey together. If serving pie warm, place whipped cream in a bowl and serve separately. If serving the pie cold, pipe the cream on top of the pie.

Note: Extra berries may be served either piled on top or in a side dish. Any flavoured honey may be whipped through cream.

SERVES 6

Australian honeys are flavoured with the nectar from both native trees and bushes and from imported plants such as lavender, giving each honey its own wonderful flavour.

Stuffed Pork Ribs with Cherry Sauce

pork spare ribs in one piece (approx 12 ribs)

MARINADE
1/4 cup/60 ml/2 fl oz light soy sauce
1 tablespoon white wine or sherry
1 tablespoon honey
1 tablespoon brown sugar
1 clove garlic, crushed
1/2 teaspoon cinnamon

STUFFING
2 cups/120 g/4 oz fresh breadcrumbs
1/2 teaspoon dried basil
2 tablespoons chopped fresh parsley
1 small onion, peeled and diced
2 tablespoons corn kernels
1 stick celery, diced
1 egg, beaten
marinade liquid
Cherry Sauce, Potato Nests, Snow Peas and Baby Corn (see recipes below), to serve

❦ Combine all marinade ingredients and marinate ribs for one hour, or overnight in the refrigerator. Turn occasionally.
❦ Preheat oven to moderate/180°C/375°F. Stand ribs in a baking pan to form a circle, secure with 2 skewers and brush both sides with marinade. Pack the stuffing in tightly. Bake for 45 minutes or until the pork is crisp looking and brown on the outside.
❦ To prepare the stuffing, combine all dry ingredients, stir in egg and sufficient marinade liquid to make the stuffing moist.
❦ To serve, place pork in centre of a large plate, surround with potato nests filled with cherries, arrange snow peas and baby corn around potato nests. Pour a little cherry sauce over the stuffing and serve remaining sauce in a jug.
❦ Serve hot (return to oven for 5 minutes if necessary to reheat).

SERVES 6

Cherry Sauce

425 g/12-14 oz can cherries, stoneless
1 teaspoon finely grated fresh ginger
1 tablespoon arrowroot
1/2 lemon
1/2 teaspoon freshly ground pepper

❦ Reserve 12 cherries for garnish. Combine remaining cherries, syrup and ginger, blend or process until smooth. Add a little of the cherry juice to arrowroot in a cup, stir until smooth. Place arrowroot in a pan and stir in remaining cherry juice with juice and grated rind (zest) of lemon.
❦ Bring to boil, stirring all the time until mixture thickens. Add pepper. Pour sauce into a jug.

Potato Nests

1 egg, beaten
1 tablespoon warm milk
2 cups warm, dry mashed potatoes

❦ Preheat oven to moderate/180°C/375°F.
❦ Combine egg and milk, pour all but 2 teaspoons into potato. Beat until potato is smooth adding a little extra milk if necessary, making sure there are no lumps. Spoon into piping bag fitted with a large star nozzle, and pipe 6 rounds onto a greased oven tray. Pipe a second layer on top to give height.
❦ Brush with the leftover egg and milk. Bake until

PEACH MELBA

rounds are lightly tipped with brown, approximately 8–10 minutes. Carefully arrange nests around the pork and place 2 cherries in each nest.

Note: Dry potato flakes mixed according to directions on packet, to a thick, smooth consistency are very easy to pipe.

SNOW PEAS, BABY CORN

12 snow peas
6 baby corn (fresh, canned or frozen)
2 teaspoons butter

❀ Wash peas, remove ends and string. Boil, steam or microwave peas and corn until just tender. Toss in butter, arrange around the potato nests.

The area around Shepparton and Euroa once provided protection for the bushranger Ned Kelly and his gang. Now it is an intensive agricultural area providing the highest quality fruits and berries for marketing and canning.

This is a classic dessert. Melba sauce will freeze for up to 6 months.

375 g/12 oz canned raspberries
squeeze lemon juice
3 scoops ice-cream
4 peach halves, canned or lightly poached
1 wafer biscuit, cut into a wedge

❀ Drain canned raspberries, retaining 2 tablespoons juice, pour the retained juice into a bowl. Push raspberries through a sieve into the bowl, discard seeds. Stir in lemon juice.

❀ To serve, place three scoops of ice-cream in dessert dishes. Arrange a peach half either side of ice-cream, pour a little chilled Melba sauce over peaches and ice-cream, top with wafer biscuit.

SERVES 1

Tree ferns, Tarra-Bulga National Park.

This dessert was created by the French chef, Georges Auguste Escoffier in 1893 and named after the famous Australian soprano, Dame Nellie Melba.

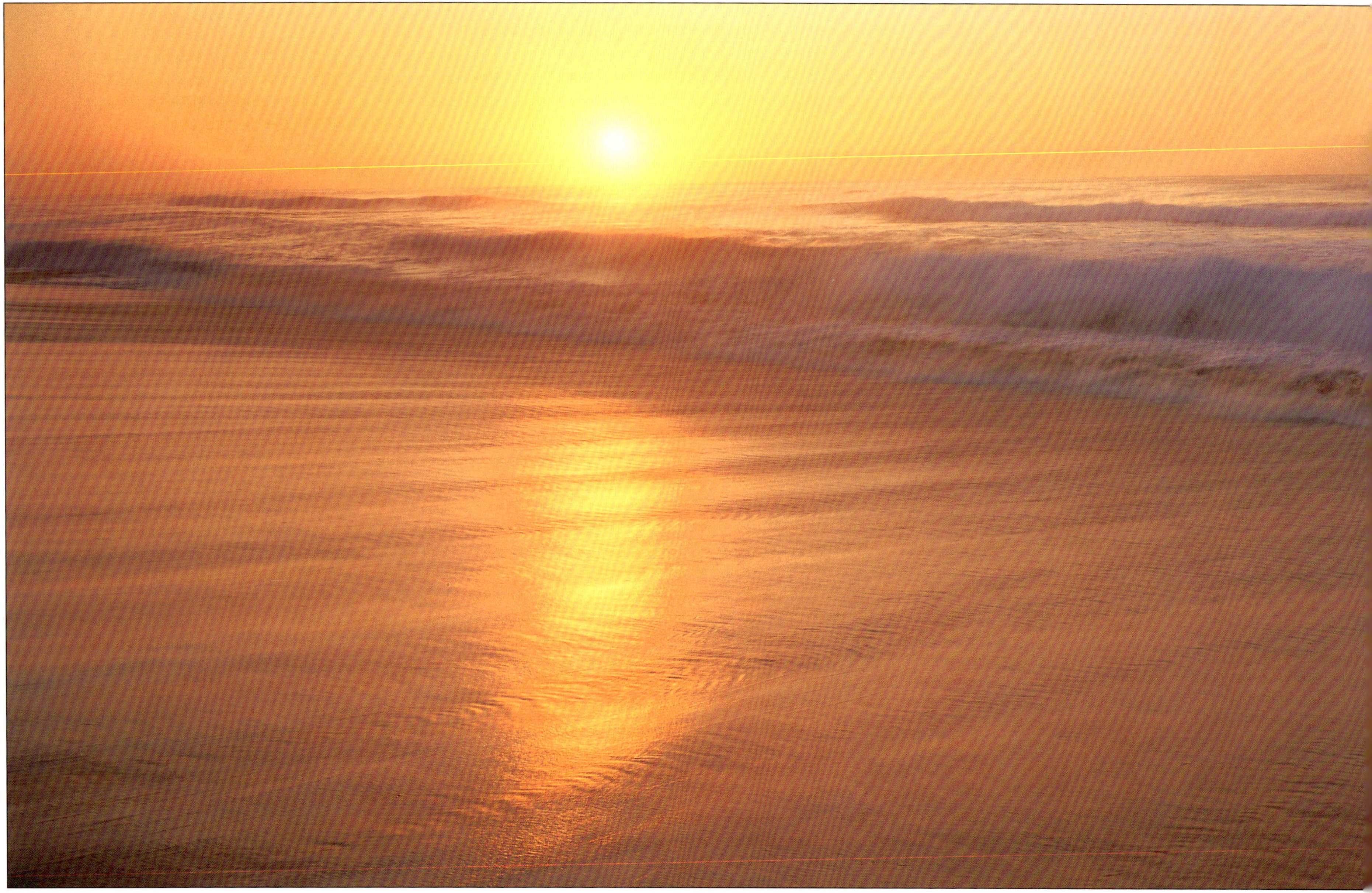

NEW SOUTH WALES

The east coast of New South Wales is rich in tracts of unspoilt bushland—here the fragrant wattle trees and tall eucalypts grow, as do the soft white flannel flowers and crimson waratahs. Along the coastline, long golden sand dunes sweep down to the rolling ocean. Inland from the coast lie lush valleys, where plantations of bananas, avocados, sugarcane and macadamia nuts grow in the rich volcanic soil.

The natural splendour offered by New South Wales, from 1900 kilometres of sun-drenched coastline to mighty inland rivers and fern-laden rainforests, is complimented by the huge array of magnificent fresh produce available. You can feast on oysters overlooking Sydney Harbour, yabbies from the Southern Highlands washed down with a fine wine from the Hunter Valley and then finish off with a wattle seed dessert from the Great Dividing Range.

Here we have presented a selection of recipes utilising some of the best ingredients from our oldest state. The variety and quality of foods on offer here is abundant—seafoods, fruits, dairy products, meats, vegetables—take your pick and savour the quality foods proudly produced in New South Wales.

A New Day, Wamberal Beach, NSW.

Sydney Rock Oysters with a Lemon Basket

allow 6-12 opened half shell oysters per serve
seafood sauce (see recipe below)
triangle of buttered bread, to garnish
parsley to garnish

❋ Arrange the opened oysters on the plate. Place seafood sauce in a lemon basket or in a small dish in the centre of plate. Surround basket with parsley. Serve immediately.

SERVES 1

Note: Crushed ice placed under the oyster plate keeps oysters chilled to perfection.

Seafood Sauce

1 tablespoon light sour cream
1 teaspoon tomato sauce
2 teaspoons mayonnaise

❋ Combine all ingredients, chill.

SERVES 1

Lemon Basket

1 lemon per serve

❋ Cut a thin slice from one side of lemon so it will sit firmly. Mark 1 cm/½ in wide strip across the top of fruit for a handle. Cut back to edge of fruit on both sides leaving the handle. With a sharp knife trim handle of flesh and remove flesh from inside of lemon.

Carrington Falls, Morton National Park.

> Sydney rock oysters are world famous, but contrary to their name are farmed from the south-east tip of Victoria right up the east coast and estuaries to the Queensland border. The handling of oysters is subject to rigid quality control to prevent contamination. It is rumoured that the legendary lover, Casanova, ate at least 40 oysters each morning for breakfast. Had he eaten the Sydney rock, he may have only needed 10!

Carnival of Stir-fry Vegetables with Linguini Pasta

1 tablespoon oil
1 teaspoon sesame oil
1 red capsicum, seeded, cut into thin strips
1 zucchini, cut into julienne strips
1 carrot, cut into julienne strips
2 sticks celery, cut into julienne strips
½ small cauliflower, cut into flowerets
½ small broccoli, cut into flowerets
2 green onions, white and green parts, cut into julienne strips
125 g/4 oz mushrooms, sliced thinly
½ bunch mint without stalks, chopped
½ bunch basil without stalks, chopped
cooked pasta (see recipe below)
sauce, to serve (see recipe below)

Note: Julienne strips are matchstick thick vegetable strips approximately 10 cm/4 in long.

❀ Heat oil and sesame oil in a large pan. Stir in capsicum, zucchini, carrot, celery, cauliflower, broccoli, green onions and mushrooms for 2 minutes. Add mint and basil, stir a further 1 minute.
❀ Add cooked pasta and sauce and toss through.
❀ Serve immediately.

PASTA

4 cups/1 litre/32 fl oz water
1 chicken stock cube
1 teaspoon oil
125 g/4 oz linguini or angel hair pasta

❀ Bring water, chicken stock cube and oil to the boil. Add pasta and bring back to boiling point. Boil 2 minutes, drain.

SAUCE

½ cup/125 ml/4 fl oz oil
juice of 1 lime
¼ cup/60 ml/2 fl oz dark soy sauce
¼ cup/60 ml/2 fl oz fish sauce
2 teaspoons brown sugar

❀ Combine all ingredients in a screw top jar, shake well to mix.

SERVES 6

Stir-fry was introduced to Australia by the Chinese who originally created the quick-fry method to conserve fuel. The food is cut into thin strips and cooked in a small quantity of oil over a high heat. This method seals in the nutrients while retaining the crispness of the food, essential in Chinese cooking.

Wattle Seed Ice-cream with Macadamia Tuiles

6 eggs
1 cup/250 g/ 8 oz sugar
600 ml/1 pt cream
¼ cup/60 ml/2 fl oz wattle seed essence

❋ Combine eggs and sugar in a heat proof bowl, whisk until thick, add cream and simmer over boiling water until thick. If you prefer to cook in a microwave, whisk eggs and sugar together. Cook on LOW 3 minutes, whisk well, add cream.
❋ Cool slightly, stir in essence*.
❋ Place in a mould or plastic bowl and freeze. When frozen break into chunks and beat with an electric beater until thick. Refreeze.
❋ To serve, scoop into a bowl and garnish with a tuile.

*If using an ice-cream maker follow manufacturer's directions from this point.

SERVES 6

> Wattle seed is made from the roasted seed of one species of wattle, and is harvested from the Great Dividing Range. It is also used to flavour bread, pasta and drinks and can be substituted for coffee.

ESSENCE

¼ cup/60 g/ 2 oz wattle seed
½ cup/125 ml/4 fl oz water

❋ Place seeds and water in a pan and simmer until liquid is reduced by half. Strain, retaining liquid and 1 tablespoon of the seeds, discard remaining seeds.

Note: ¼ cup/60 ml/2 fl oz strong black coffee and 2 teaspoons finely crushed hazelnuts may be substituted for wattle seed essence and seeds.

Macadamia Tuiles

1 egg white
¼ cup/60 g/2 oz sugar
2 tablespoons plain flour
20 g/½ oz butter, melted
½ teaspoon vanilla essence
2 tablespoons crushed macadamia nuts

❋ Preheat oven to moderate/180°C/375°F.
❋ Whisk egg white until stiff, gradually add the sugar. Fold in flour, butter and essence. Place 1 teaspoonful of mixture on a greased oven tray.
❋ Using the back of a spoon, flatten the mixture slightly and sprinkle with a little of the crushed nuts. Repeat until tray is full. Bake 5 minutes, or until tuile has started to turn golden, (only bake one tray at a time).
❋ With a spatula or egg slice, carefully remove tuile from tray and drape over a rolling pin to cool.
❋ Continue with rest of mixture.

Will keep in an airtight container in the refrigerator for several weeks. If tuile softens re-bake in a moderate oven 3 minutes, and cool over the rolling pin.

MAKES APPROXIMATELY 15

Fisherman, Terrigal Beach.

NEW SOUTH WALES 19

Yabbies in Green Coats

If using cooked yabbies follow recipe from*.

24 green (uncooked) yabbies

STOCK

3 cups/750 ml/24 fl oz water

juice of 1 lemon

1 bay leaf

6 parsley stalks with leaves

1 stick celery, diced

1 small carrot, diced

2 teaspoons powdered chicken stock

dill sprigs, to garnish

❀ Cover yabbies in fresh water, allow to stand at least 4 hours, changing water twice. Drain.
❀ Combine all ingredients for stock in a deep pan bring to boil and simmer 20 minutes. Add yabbies, simmer 5 minutes, drain, discarding stock.
*Keep 6 whole cooked yabbies, to garnish.
❀ Remove flesh from the tails of remaining 18 yabbies, place in a bowl, discard shells.

> Yabby is the Aboriginal name for small, freshwater crayfish. In times of drought the yabby digs a burrow emerging only when the creek or dam refills.

PASTRY SHELLS

2 sheets commercial puff pastry

1 egg, beaten

❀ Preheat oven to hot/250°C/475°F.
❀ Cut 12 circles in a shell shape, approximately 6cm/ 2½ in wide. To achieve a defined shell, use the back of a scallop shell that has been greased.
❀ Place on a greased oven tray, brush with egg. Bake in oven until pastry is golden brown. Remove from oven.

MAYONNAISE

2 large avocados

1 x 400 g/13 oz can condensed milk

½ teaspoon English (hot) dry mustard

2 tablespoons brown vinegar

1 teaspoon lemon juice

dash salt, pepper

❀ Peel avocados, remove stones, place in a bowl and mash. Combine all other ingredients for mayonnaise with avocado pulp, mix well. Add yabbies and coat well with mayonnaise.
❀ To assemble, place 1 pastry shell on a plate. Heat yabbies in mayonnaise by stirring over a low heat. If you prefer to cook in a microwave, cook on HIGH 1 minute.
❀ Spoon mayonnaise into shell with 3 of the coated yabbies. Top with a pastry shell. Repeat. Garnish with dill sprig and 1 whole yabby per serve.

SERVES 6

Note: Plain commercial or homemade mayonnaise may be used.

Lamb in Macadamia Crust with Mango Jus

2 lamb cutlets
1 egg yolk
2 tablespoons water
125 g/4 oz macadamia nuts, crushed coarsely
1 cup/125 g/4 oz dried breadcrumbs
oil for shallow frying

JUS
pulp of 2 mangoes
1 teaspoon chicken stock powder
2 tablespoons water
1 tablespoon chopped parsley, to garnish

❦ Trim cutlet bone of fat and skin. Flatten cutlet meat. Beat egg yolk and water together in a shallow dish, dip each side of cutlet in the mixture. In a plastic bag mix nuts and breadcrumbs. Drop cutlets, one at a time, into bag, shake to coat meat with crumbs. Repeat with each cutlet. Heat oil and fry cutlets 2 minutes each side. Drain on absorbent paper. Keep hot.

❦ To make the jus, combine all ingredients, heat.

❦ To serve, place 2 cutlets on each serving plate, spoon a little jus around meat. Garnish with parsley.

SERVES 6

> Macadamia nuts were known to the Aboriginal people as 'Kindal-Kindal' or 'Baphal' for thousands of years. They were first discovered by European settlers in 1800 and named after the Melbourne scientist, John Macadam.

Old homestead, Silverton.

Bananas in Chocolate Mud

3 bananas, peeled
2 tablespoons butter, melted
1 tablespoon brandy
3 tablespoons brown sugar
chocolate mud sauce (see recipe below)
2 tablespoons shaved chocolate, whipped cream and strawberries, to garnish

❊ Preheat oven to moderate/180°C/375°F.
❊ Place whole, peeled bananas in an ovenproof dish. Combine melted butter, brandy and brown sugar together in a pan, stir until sugar has dissolved. Pour over bananas and bake in oven 10 minutes.
❊ If you prefer to cook in a microwave, place bananas in a dish, pour over mixture, cook on HIGH 3 minutes.

Chocolate Mud Sauce

250 g/8 oz dark chocolate pieces
20 g/½ oz butter
1 drop vanilla essence
2 tablespoons light sour cream

❊ Melt chocolate over pan of hot water, stir in butter, remove from heat and add vanilla and sour cream.
❊ If you prefer to cook in a microwave, combine chocolate, butter and vanilla in a bowl, cook on HIGH 1–2 minutes, stir until chocolate melts, add cream.
❊ To serve, pour chocolate mixture into serving dish. Carefully lift 1 banana into each serving dish, spoon over a little of the butter mixture. Top with whipped cream and shaved chocolate and a strawberry.
❊ Serve while warm.

SERVES 3

Note: Brown sugar is a moist sugar as a portion of the refining syrup is retained during the production process which gives it its distinctive flavour and colour.

Flame tree, Bombaderry.

Bananas are an introduced crop to Northern New South Wales, but a most important one. The annual crop yields approximately 152 000 tonnes. It is not uncommon to see banana trees festooned with blue plastic bags. The plastic protects the bunches from sunburn while increasing yields and quality. The average bunch weighs between 25–45 kilos. Bananas are one of the first fruit introduced to a baby's diet, as once ripe, they are easily digested.

POWDER PUFFS

3 large eggs, separated
¾ cup/165 g/5½ oz caster sugar
¾ cup/95 g/3 oz cornflour
¼ cup/30 g/1 oz plain flour
½ teaspoon bicarbonate of soda
2 teaspoons boiling water
whipped cream
sifted icing sugar, to garnish

❀ Preheat oven to moderate/180°C/375°F.
❀ Whip egg whites until stiff. Beat in egg yolks and add sugar, 1 tablespoon at a time, beating well between each addition. Sift flours and bicarbonate together, fold into mixture then add boiling water.
❀ Place dessertspoons of mixture onto the first of 3 greased oven trays, allowing the mixture to spread. Place first tray in oven before spooning mixture onto second tray.
❀ Place second tray in oven then repeat for third tray.
❀ Bake 8–10 minutes or until puffs are golden brown. Remove puffs immediately from trays with a spatula and cool on wire rack, (if puffs crinkle when removing from trays allow another minute to cook).
❀ To serve, join cold puffs together with whipped cream, and dust with icing sugar. If desired, a little jam can be used with the cream to join. Allow to stand 1 hour before serving to allow puffs to soften.

MAKES 24

> Australian country women are renowned for their light sponge cakes, filled with cream and dusted with icing sugar. The 'Powder Puff' or 'Sponge Kiss' is a small variation of the larger sponge and is thought to have originated when too much mixture was made for the sponge tins, so the leftover mixture was spooned onto trays, cooked and no doubt eaten by the cook and her 'helpers' with a cup of hot tea as soon as the baking was done.

Sand dunes.

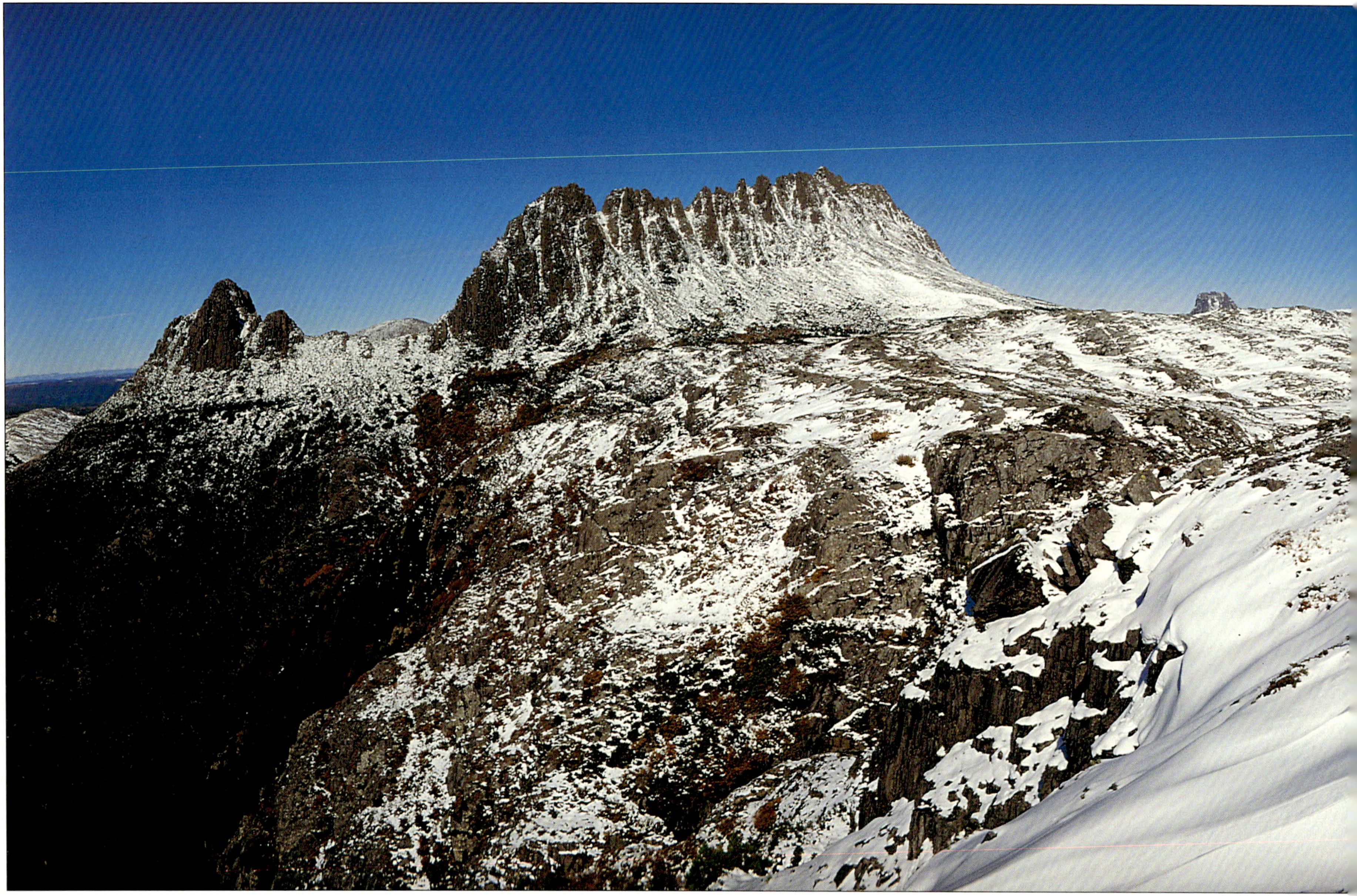

Tasmania

Cross Bass Strait and you reach the delightful island of Tasmania. Formerly known as Van Dieman's land, but named in 1855 after Abel Tasman, this island state is only 68 000 square kilometres. However, the old adage of good things coming in small packages has never been more true. Tasmania is home to some of Australia's greatest and most respected produce.

Here you can feast on the most delicious crayfish and scallops scooped fresh from coves of pure white sand. The Tasmanian trout and salmon are also superb, having been bred in the pristine waters of the many magnificent rivers here. In Tasmania you can enjoy the best of both worlds—breathtaking scenery and a superb variety of fresh food.

Imagine walking alongside Dove Lake, the striking sight of Cradle Mountain reflected in the crystal clear waters, then returning to a steaming hot pot of potato soup to welcome you inside from the fresh, cool air. Read on!

Snowdrift, Cradle Mountain, TAS.

POTATO SOUP WITH GARLIC CROUTONS

20 g/½ oz butter
2 spring onions, peeled, finely diced
3 large potatoes, peeled and sliced
2 chicken stock cubes
2 cups/500 ml/16 fl oz water
300 ml/10 fl oz cream
chopped parsley, to garnish

❧ In a deep pan, melt butter and fry onions until transparent, add potatoes, stock cubes and water. Bring to boil, simmer 40 minutes. Cool slightly, blend or process until liquidised. When ready to serve, add cream and reheat without boiling. Ladle into soup bowls, sprinkle with parsley and garlic croutons.

SERVES 4

CROUTONS
3 slices bread, crusts removed
2 cloves garlic, crushed
¼ cup/60 ml/2 fl oz oil

❧ Cut bread into small squares or small, fancy shapes. Combine garlic and oil in a large screw top jar, add bread and toss until bread is covered with oil. Croutons can be either baked or fried. When totally cold, store in an airtight container, will stay fresh for several weeks.

❧ To bake: place on an oven tray in a moderate oven (about 180°C/375°F). Cook croutons, moving them occasionally until bread cubes are brown. Drain and cool thoroughly.

❧ To fry: heat oil or fat for shallow frying. Cook bread cubes until brown, drain. Cool thoroughly.

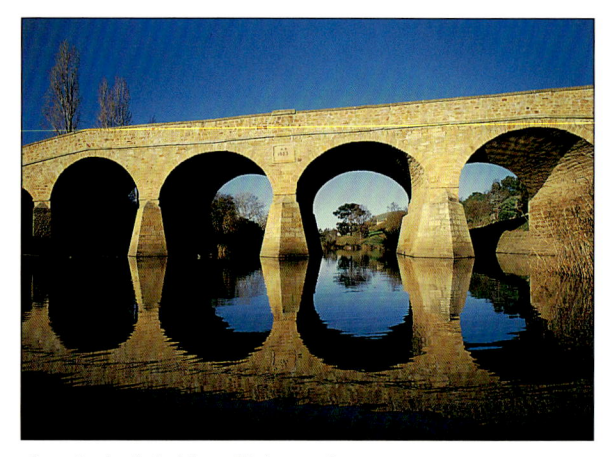

Convict built bridge, Richmond.

Potato growing in Australia was reputed to have started with the first farm established by Governor Phillip in 1788. In a report written by him in 1791, he mentioned that two acres were under potato. Tasmania soon became an early provider and in 1830 the cutter *Fanny* brought the first shipment of 46 tons to the Australian mainland. Unlike most other countries, Australia can provide a fresh harvest of potatoes all year round.

POACHED TASMANIAN TROUT WITH LEMON ALMONDS

1 fillet of white fish
1/4 cup/60 ml/2 fl oz white wine
1 bay leaf
3 peppercorns
6 fresh coriander leaves
1 small onion, peeled and diced
1 cup/250 ml/8 fl oz water
3 medium sized trout, cleaned
1 tablespoon almond flakes
20 g/ 1/2 oz butter
juice of 1 lemon
1 lemon and 1 dill, to garnish

❁ Preheat oven to moderate/180°C/375°F.
❁ Combine fish fillet, wine, bay leaf, peppercorns, coriander, onion and water in a covered pan, bring to boil and allow to simmer for 20 minutes. Drain retaining the stock, discarding the solids.
❁ Wash trout, pat dry and place side by side in ovenproof dish.
❁ Pour the fish stock over the trout. Cover trout and stock with a lid or greased foil. Bake 20–25 minutes or until fish is tender.
❁ Place almonds and butter in a pan over heat, stir until almonds are golden, add lemon juice.
❁ Carefully lift trout onto 3 warmed serving plates.
❁ Leaving the head and tail on, remove skin from body. Mix a little of the fish stock in the pan with the almonds and juice and pour over the trout.
❁ Serve trout whilst hot, garnished with lemon slices and dill.

SERVES 3

> Trout farming was established in Tasmania nearly 160 years ago. The original trout eggs were carried in billy cans on horseback, before being put into the inland lakes to hatch. They are now bred in salmon ponds close to the inland waterways before being released. The number of trout caught is strictly controlled by licensing.

Uniting Church, Penguin.

Cradle Mountain Apple

6 green apples, washed and cored
2 tablespoons water
2 tablespoons brown sugar
40 g/1½ oz soft butter
½ teaspoon ground cinnamon
1 tablespoon sultanas
5 egg whites
5 tablespoons caster sugar

❀ Preheat oven to moderate/180°C/375°F.
❀ Place apples in a baking dish with water. Beat brown sugar and butter together until creamy.
❀ Add cinnamon and sultanas. Push the mixture into the apple cavity. Bake for 20 minutes or until apples are tender. If you prefer to cook in a microwave, cook on HIGH 6–8 minutes, allow to stand 1 minute. Test for tenderness.
❀ Allow to cool slightly.
❀ Whip egg whites until stiff, gradually add the caster sugar a spoonful at a time. Remove apples from baking dish and place on a greased oven tray. With a flat knife, thickly spread meringue around each apple, covering totally. Bake until meringue starts to brown slightly.
❀ Serve immediately.

SERVES 6

Liffey Falls.

> The first apple orchard in Huonville was planted in 1841 and the fruit was exported in 1849 to India and New Zealand. In the years between the two World Wars, 500 different varieties of apples were grown, but since then the number has reduced to about eight.

Scallops with Cheesy Topping

18 fresh scallops
1 cup/250 ml/8 fl oz milk
1 tablespoon white wine
1 tablespoon cream
1 tablespoon finely diced green onion
½ teaspoon French mustard
4 slices bread
1 tablespoon grated tasty or cheddar cheese

❀ Marinate the scallops in milk for at least 4 hours, or longer. The milk 'plumps' and tenderises the scallop.

❀ Preheat the griller. Lightly grease 3 small oven-proof or scallop shell dishes. Drain the scallops, retaining two tablespoons of milk. With a sharp knife cut the coral away from the scallop and chop the coral. Place 6 scallops and coral in each dish.

❀ Mix the reserved 2 tablespoons of milk with wine, cream, green onions and French mustard and heat until just warm. Pour equally over scallops.

❀ Remove crusts from bread and grate or crumble bread to make fine crumbs. Mix with cheese. Top the scallops with the bread mixture and brown under a griller.

❀ Serve immediately from griller.

SERVES 3

Orange willow, Deloraine.

Scallops can often be purchased still in their pretty orange-brown fluted shell. They prefer to live on a silty sandy gravel bed in coastal bays, and are usually available all year. The scallop is very delicate and should only be cooked 3–5 minutes and not reheated.

Overleaf: *Cannonball, TAS.*

TASMANIA 29

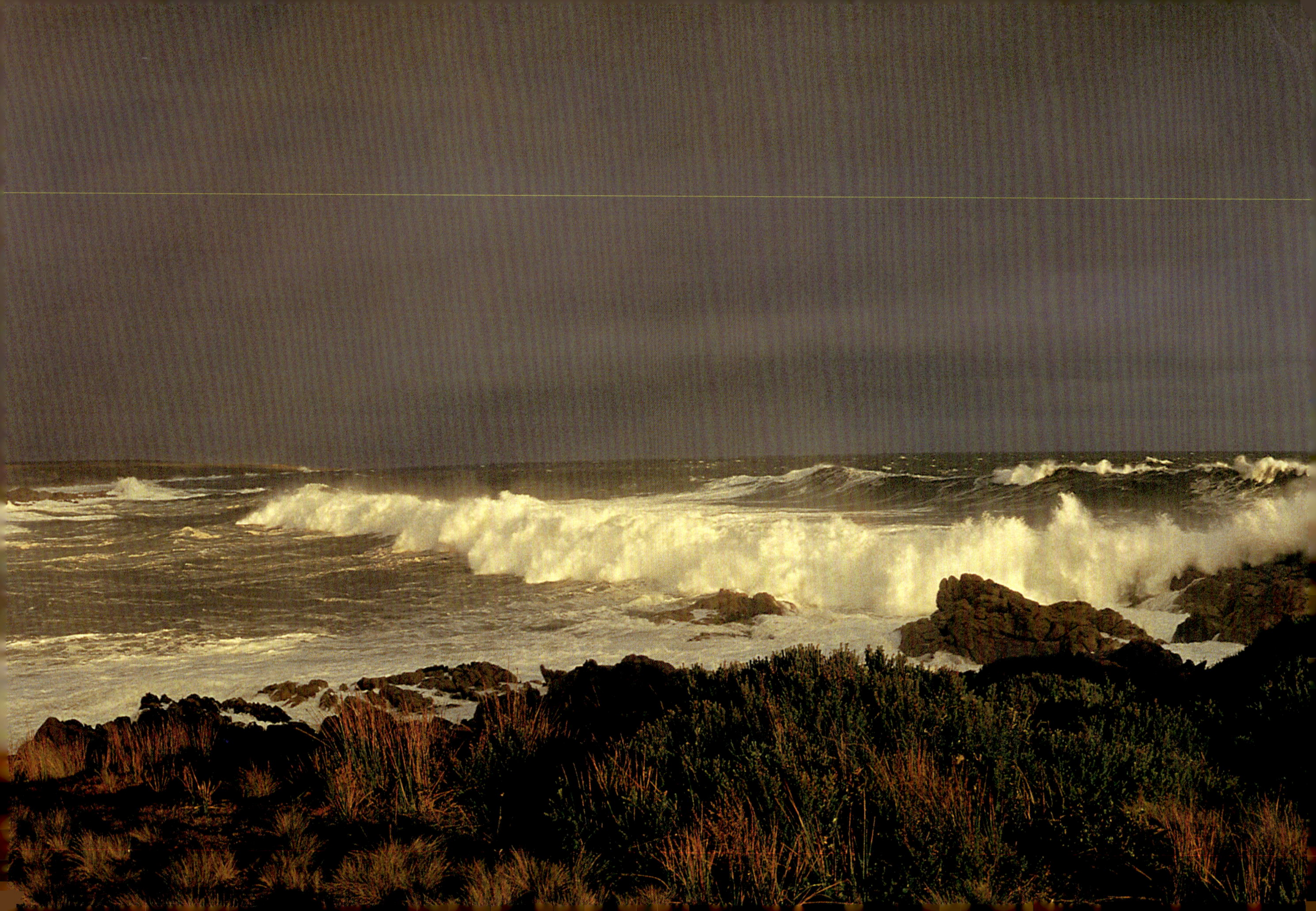

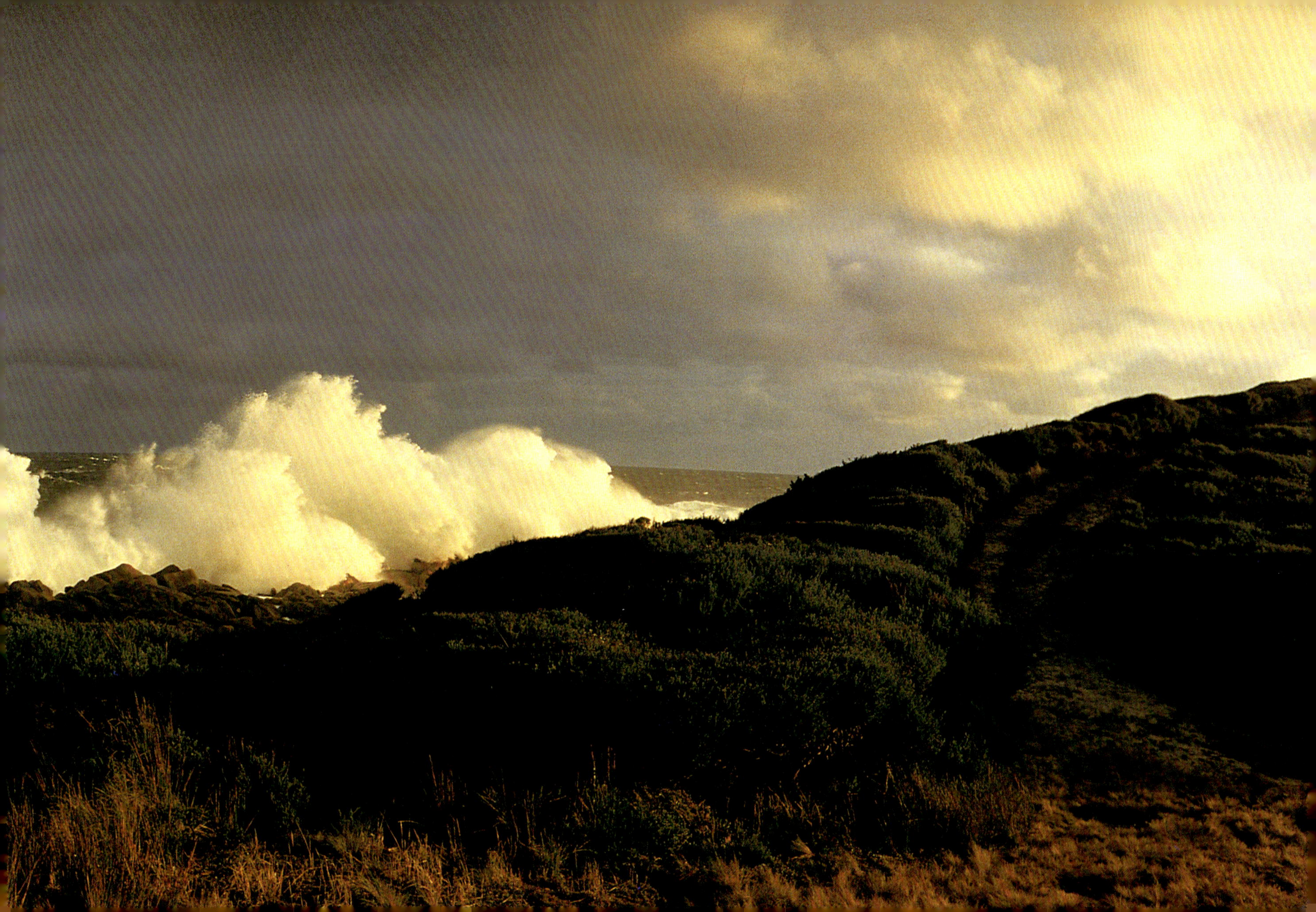

Smoked Salmon Wrapped in Potato Crepe with a Coulis Duet

CREPE
2 potatoes, peeled and cooked
20 g/½ oz butter, melted
1 egg, beaten
1 tablespoon milk
1 tablespoon plain flour
extra butter

FILLING
1–2 teaspoons horseradish sauce, to taste
1 tablespoon finely chopped onion
4 tablespoons thick sour cream
3 slices smoked salmon
1 slice smoked salmon, extra, cut into very thin strips and rolled and sprigs of dill, to garnish

❊ To prepare the crepe, mash potatoes, melted butter, egg, milk and flour together. Allow to stand 1 hour.

❊ Melt extra butter in a frying pan, bring it to sizzling point. Pour 1 tablespoon of the mixture into the pan, tilt pan so the mixture spreads to form a thin circle. Allow to cook for 1 minute. Lift a little of the crepe up to see if the underneath is brown, if so turn and brown the other side.

❊ Repeat until all mixture is used, add a little more of the extra butter to keep the pan lightly greased. As each crepe is cooked, place it in a damp tea towel to keep soft, or between layers of damp greaseproof paper.

❊ To prepare the filling, combine horseradish, onion and sour cream together, mix well. Spread a thin layer of the cream over one side of the crepe.

❊ Place a single layer of smoked salmon on top of the cream and roll up firmly. Refrigerate until the coulis is prepared or until ready to serve (can be made the day before).

❊ To serve, cut the crepe roll approximately 8 cm/ 3 in long. Place on entree dish and spoon cucumber coulis on one side and capsicum coulis on the other.

❊ Garnish with extra smoked salmon rolls and dill.

Note: This crepe mixture is a little difficult to handle, but is worth persevering with, however, a plain crepe mixture may be used. If on standing, the crepe mixture becomes too thick, add a little milk to return mixture to a thick cream consistency.

SERVES 6-8 (depending on size of crepes)

Dove Lake, Cradle Mountain.

CRAYFISH FRESHLY GRILLED WITH LEMON BUTTER

COULIS DUET

CUCUMBER

1 green cucumber, peeled and sliced in half with the seeds removed
$1/2$ teaspoon salt
$1/2$ tablespoon fresh mint, without stems
$1/2$ cup/125 ml/4 fl oz natural yoghurt
1 teaspoon sugar
squeeze lemon or lime juice

❦ Sprinkle cucumber with salt, place in a strainer or on absorbent towel for 3 minutes. Rinse under cold water. Combine all ingredients in a blender or processor, process to form a thick liquid.

CAPSICUM

1 red capsicum, cut in half with seeds removed, rinsed
1 small onion, diced
$1/4$ cup/60 ml/2 fl oz water

❦ Preheat oven to moderate/180°C/375°F.
❦ Place capsicum in oven and roast until the skin starts to brown. Cool slightly and remove skin. Place capsicum and other ingredients in a blender or processor and process until liquidised.

SERVES 6-8 (depending on size of crepes)

---

1 fresh crayfish (green)
80 g/$2 1/2$ oz butter
juice of 1 lemon
$1/2$ teaspoon freshly ground pepper
Preheat your griller or barbecue.

❦ Cut crayfish in half, rinse lightly in cold water.
❦ Melt butter, add lemon juice and pepper, pour over crayfish. Grill or barbecue crays until tail meat just turns white.
❦ Serve hot or cold.

SERVES 2

Grass and sand dunes.

'Nubeena' is the Aboriginal word for crayfish. The sea-crayfish are exported as Australian lobster or rock lobster. There are many species of cray found in freshwater dams, swamps, waterholes as well as in the sea.

Mussels Swimming in Garlic and Brandy

12 mussels, opened
½ cup/125 g/4 oz butter, melted
3 cloves garlic, crushed
1 tablespoon brandy
1 tablespoon finely chopped parsley, to garnish

❧ Preheat your griller or barbecue.
❧ Place mussels on an oven tray. Combine butter, garlic and brandy and pour over mussels. Place under griller or on a BBQ and cook until butter sizzles.
❧ Sprinkle with parsley and serve while hot.

SERVES 2

Note: If mussels are bought unopened, cook by covering them with water and bringing to the boil, removing mussels as soon as they open. When the majority are cooked discard any unopened mussels. If you prefer, microwave mussels in microwave oven. Cook on HIGH removing mussels as they open. Discard any unopened mussels.

> Mussels are often eaten in place of the more expensive oyster. Previously collected at low tide, they are now being farmed by using rafts with long ropes attached. The ropes are 'seeded' with mussels then suspended in water. If cooking unopened mussels, they should be well scrubbed, the beard should be cut off and they should be stood in clean water for a few hours to rid themselves of grit and sand. Once cooked, any unopened mussels should be discarded as being stale.

Organ Pipes, Mt Wellington.

34 TASMANIA

Apple and Caraway Seed Bread with Cheeses

1 apple, peeled and cored
1 tablespoon water
3 egg whites
½ cup/110 g/3½ oz caster sugar
1 cup/125 g/4 oz plain flour
1 tablespoon caraway seeds
assorted cheeses, to serve

❋ Preheat oven to moderate/180°C/375°F.
❋ Slice apples very thinly and gently cook in water until tender, drain. If you prefer to cook in a microwave, cook apples and water on HIGH 2 minutes, test for tenderness.
❋ Whip egg whites until stiff, gradually beat in the sugar. Fold in flour and caraway seeds, carefully stir in apples.
❋ Spoon mixture into greased and lined 25 cm x 8 cm/10 in x 3 in bar tin and bake 30–35 minutes, or until firm to touch. Turn out, remove paper and allow to cool thoroughly. When cold, wrap in foil and chill for at least 24 hours.

Note: This bread must be made a day or more before the second baking.

Second Baking

❋ Preheat oven to very slow/120°C/250°F.
❋ Use a sharp knife and cut bread into wafer-thin slices. Place on a greased oven tray and bake until dry and crisp.
❋ To serve, arrange bread slices on a platter with cheeses and serve after dinner with coffee.

> Cheese is made from different milks. The unique flavour of cheese often stems from the grasses or fodder fed to the cows, hence cheeses from different parts of Australia have distinct flavours. Cheese making has, up until recent times, followed European styles. Now however, cheese makers are developing styles of cheese to suit our own tastes and requirements.

Farm cottage, Campbell.

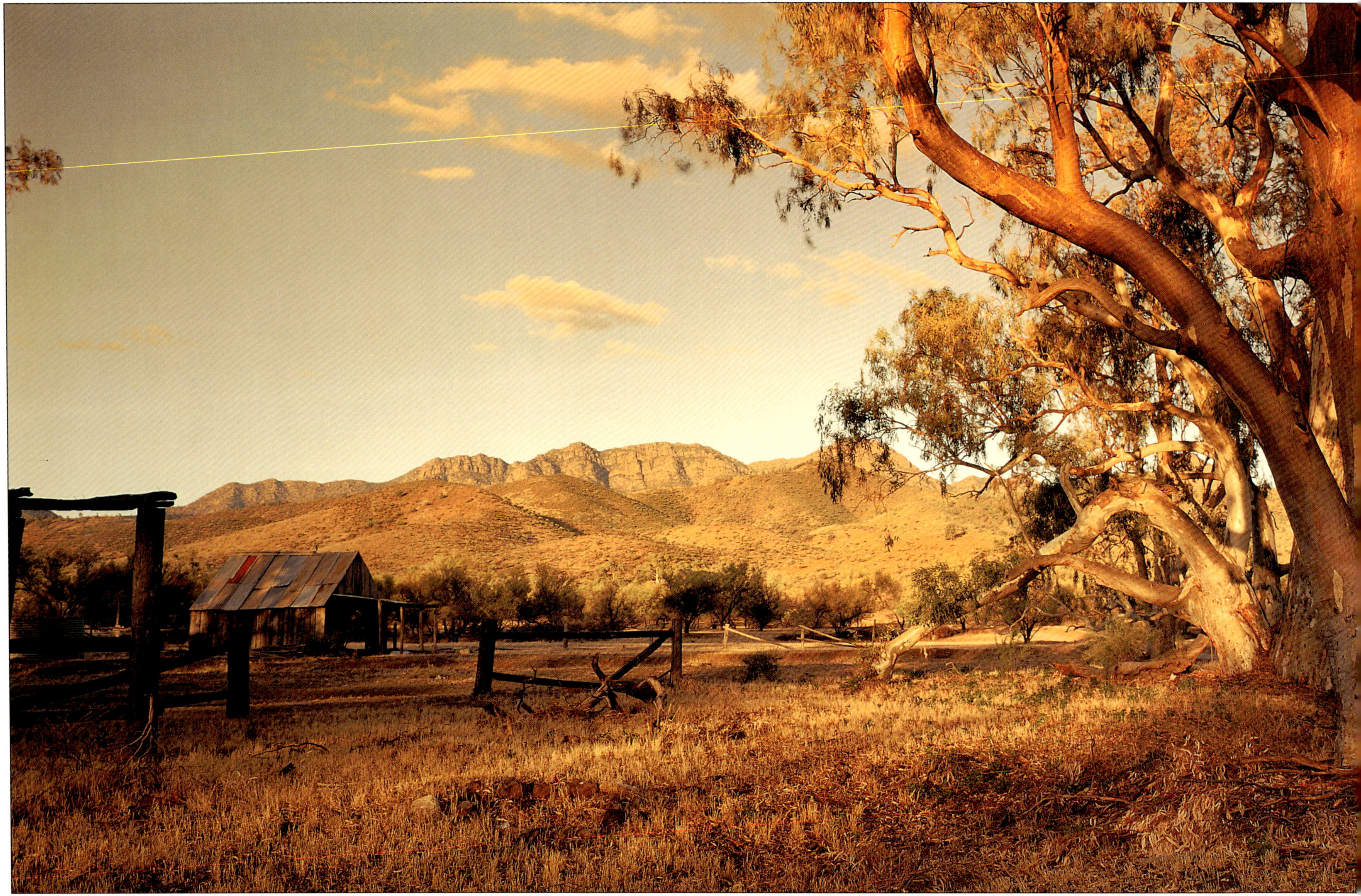

SOUTH AUSTRALIA

The glorious climate in South Australia meant that the early settlers of this state were very enthusiastic about eating outdoors. The picnic is still everyone's favourite pastime here. Where better to enjoy lunch (and the superb wines of the Barossa Valley!) than in the wildflower-strewn valleys of the dramatic Flinders Ranges? At over 400 kilometres in length, the ranges offer endless opportunities to experience the beauty that is South Australia. Fill your hamper with fresh asparagus drizzled with walnut dressing or quail with a Mediterranean flavour mirroring the multicultural history of this state.

Sites like this of the Flinders Ranges have drawn travellers from afar to admire their majesty.

You could easily spend many hours dreaming in this extraordinarily beautiful spot, contemplating the dramatic mountain peaks and deep, shady gorges . . .

Flinders Ranges, SA.

Kangaroo 'n Beer

1½ kg/3 lb kangaroo meat, cut into 2.5 cm/1 in cubes (round or chuck steak may be substituted for kangaroo)
2 onions, thinly sliced
2 potatoes, peeled, cut into 2.5 cm/1 in cubes
1 tablespoon plain flour
pinch dried mixed herbs
1 beef stock cube
375 ml/12 fl oz beer
375 ml/12 fl oz water
French loaf bread, sliced in 2.5 cm/1 in thick slices
French mustard
1 cup grated cheese

❦ Preheat oven to moderate/180°C/375°F.
❦ Toss meat, onions and potatoes in combined flour, herbs and crumbled stock cube. Place in a casserole dish, add the beer and water. Cover and cook in oven for 1½ hours.
❦ When casserole is cooked, spread bread slices with French mustard. Place bread, mustard side up, on top of casserole and press lightly into gravy, sprinkle with cheese. Return to oven and allow cheese to melt.
❦ To serve, spoon casserole with topping onto warmed plates.
❦ This is a tasty casserole. It will freeze, without the topping for 3 months.

SERVES 6

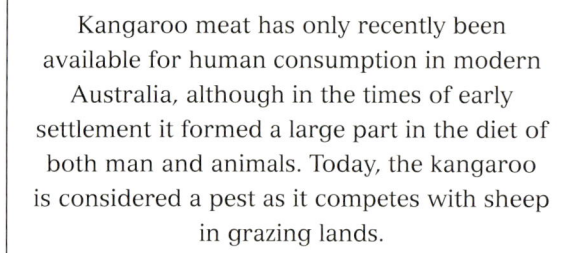

Rattlin' Annie, Cummins.

> Kangaroo meat has only recently been available for human consumption in modern Australia, although in the times of early settlement it formed a large part in the diet of both man and animals. Today, the kangaroo is considered a pest as it competes with sheep in grazing lands.

Pears Poached in Red Wine with a Fresh Fig Custard

Pears will have a richer colour if allowed to marinate before cooking. Cover or turn the pears regularly in the marinade.

6 firm pears
1 cup/250 ml/8 fl oz red wine
½ cup/125 ml/4 fl oz water
1 tablespoon sugar
2 cloves or ½ teaspoon ground cloves

❦ Carefully peel pears leaving stalk attached. Place upright in a pan. Combine wine, water, sugar and cloves, pour over pears. Bring to boil and allow to simmer until pears are tender but not too soft.
❦ During this time, baste pears to allow the syrup to colour the fruit.
❦ If you prefer to use a microwave, cook pears on HIGH 4 minutes, turn pears over cook a further 4 minutes on HIGH, test for tenderness.
❦ To serve, place pears upright in a bowl, brush pears with a little of the wine syrup. Pour fig custard around the pears. Garnish with fig halves. Serve warm.

SERVES 6

Fig Custard

2 fresh figs
1 cup/250 ml/8 fl oz milk
1 tablespoon sugar
1 egg, separated
fresh figs, to garnish

❦ Peel and puree the figs. In a pan, heat milk until almost simmering, remove from heat. Beat egg yolk and sugar together, stir into milk. Return milk to heat and stir, without boiling, until mixture thickens.

❦ If you prefer to use a microwave, combine milk, sugar and egg yolk, beat. Cook on SLOW or MEDIUM, for 2 minutes, beat well. Cook a further 2 minutes, beat well, allow to stand for 2 minutes. If custard is not sufficiently thick, cook a further 1–2 minutes, beating well.
❦ Whip egg white until stiff, fold into custard with fig puree.

Wine is one of the oldest beverages known and results from the fermentation of grapes. The colour of the wine comes from the particular grape used in fermentation. Five states of Australia vie with each other in producing the best wines. Each of these states are producing high quality wines recognised throughout the world for their distinctive flavours.

Quail with Olives and Sun-dried Tomato

¼ cup sun-dried tomatoes in oil
¼ cup olives, stoned
1 tablespoon chopped parsley
1 tablespoon chopped basil
extra oil, if necessary
4 quails, cleaned
4 chive strips, to serve
1 cup rice, cooked and kept hot
lightly cooked broccoli, cherry tomatoes, to garnish

❀ Preheat oven to moderate/180°C/375°F.
❀ Chop tomatoes and olives, place in a dish, add ½ cup/125 ml/4 fl oz tomato oil (make up tomato oil quantity with extra oil if necessary). Stir in remaining ingredients. Brush the quail with the mixture and then place the quail in the bowl. Allow to stand one hour. Turn quails once or twice during this time.
❀ Remove quails from marinade and place quails on their backs in a baking dish, brush with oil from marinade. Loosely tie the legs together with string. Bake until quails are tender, approximately 30 minutes, brushing occasionally with marinade oil.
❀ Strain marinade and mix the tomatoes and olives with the hot rice.
❀ To serve, remove string from quail and tie legs with a strip of chive. Place a spoonful of rice on a plate, carefully arrange quail on rice and garnish with broccoli and cherry tomatoes.

SERVES 2

Olives were first introduced to South Australia from Rio de Janeiro in 1830. The first olive oil producing plants arrived in 1851 from Marseilles, and in the early part of the century 2300 tons of olives were being produced, however by 1940 the production of oil ceased to be profitable and oils were imported from overseas. Olive trees are found in most older established gardens in South Australia. Olives, as a fruit, are once again being cultivated and should be bottled within 8 hours of picking. There is a native olive found in the Northern Territory which contains the highest level of vitamin C of any plant.

Innes National Park, Yorke Peninsula.

Fresh Asparagus Dressed with Walnut

approximately 24 spears fresh asparagus
water
DRESSING
1 teaspoon brown sugar
1 teaspoon French mustard
dash freshly ground pepper
½ cup/125 ml/4 fl oz walnut or sesame oil
1 tablespoon vinegar
1 tablespoon walnuts, finely chopped
strip of chive, to garnish

❀ Wash asparagus in warm water, cut off 1 cm/ ½ in from end of stalks. Place in the top of a steamer.
❀ Steam until stalks are tender, approximately 15 minutes.
❀ If you prefer to use a microwave, place in a long dish, add ¼ cup/60 ml/2 fl oz water, cover with wrap. Cook on HIGH 2 minutes, allow to stand 2 minutes.
❀ To prepare the dressing, combine all ingredients for dressing in a screw topped jar, shake vigorously.
❀ To serve, drain asparagus, tie into a bundle with a chive and drizzle with walnut dressing.

SERVES 6

> Asparagus is a member of the lily family of plants. Two main varieties are grown in Australia, the white asparagus used for canning and the green asparagus as a fresh vegetable. The true walnut tree is a deciduous and umbrageous tree cultivated for its annual crop. Australia names various timbers 'walnut' from the 'laurel' family of trees.

Grass trees, Flinders Ranges.

SOUTH AUSTRALIA

Aussie Meat Pie with Tomato Sauce

This is Australia's own special dish.

FILLING
750 g/1½ lb round steak cut into 1 cm/½ in cubes (see Note 1)
1½ cups/375 ml/12 fl oz water
1 beef stock cube
salt and pepper to taste
1 onion, sliced very finely
2 tablespoons plain flour
1 teaspoon Worcestershire sauce

PIE BASE
2 cups/250 g/8 oz plain flour
pinch salt
60 g/2 oz beef dripping
⅔ cup/160 ml/5 fl oz water
extra flour

TOPPING
commercial puff pastry
extra flour
egg yolk mixed with a little milk, to glaze
tomato sauce, to serve

❈ To prepare the filling, combine all ingredients in a pan, stir until boiling. Cover, allow to simmer, stirring occasionally, for 1 hour. Cool thoroughly before using.

❈ To prepare the base, sift flour and salt into a bowl. Combine dripping and water together into a pan, stir over heat until dripping melts. Stir into flour until combined. Turn out onto a floured sheet of paper, knead slightly until smooth. Roll out and line base and sides of 8 greased 10 x cm x 10 cm/4 in x 4 in pie tins.

❈ Fill tins with meat mixture.

❈ To prepare topping, preheat oven to moderate/ 180°C/375°F.

❈ Roll puff pastry out onto a floured sheet. Cut a circle to fit tops of pie. Wet edge of pastry base with egg and milk mixture and press pie tops into place. Trim edges and press to join. Brush with egg and milk and make a small hole in centre of pie to allow steam to escape.

❈ Bake for 15–20 minutes until pies are golden brown.

❈ Serve hot with tomato sauce.

SERVES 8

Note 1: Mince steak may be substituted for round steak in this recipe. Use 750 g/1½ lb mince and 1 cup of water. Combine with other ingredients, bring to the boil and simmer for 30 minutes or microwave on HIGH for 10–15 minutes.

Note 2: Puff pastry may be used for top and bottom of pie if desired.

The Aussie meat pie is an Australian tradition through all walks of life. The actual origin seems lost but the first recorded mention of the 'pie' appeared in 1850 in the Melbourne newspaper, the *Argus*, which reported that the councillors were unhappy with the food served in the Chambers and preferred a 'pie' from the pub opposite. There would be no town in Australia where you could not buy a pie, whether pre-packaged or freshly baked, for the pie is part of our heritage.

Burra Homestead, Mount Lofty Ranges.

SOUTH AUSTRALIA 43

Fruit Crumble with Whipped Cream

125 g/4 oz mixed dried fruit (apricots, apples, prunes, pears)
2 cups/500 ml/16 fl oz hot water
½ cup/125 g/4 oz sugar

BASE
125 g/4 oz butter
125 g/4 oz sugar
1 egg
1 cup/125 g/4 oz plain flour
½ cup/60 g/2 oz self-raising flour

TOPPING
1 cup/90 g/3 oz desiccated coconut
1 cup/90 g/3 oz rolled oats or crushed cornflakes
90 g/3 oz butter
½ cup/90 g/3 oz brown sugar or 2 tablespoons honey
thick cream or ice-cream, to garnish

❦ Place dried fruits and hot water in a pan, stand for 30 minutes.
❦ Cook over heat, bring to boil, lower heat and allow to simmer, covered, 10 minutes. Add sugar, stir until dissolved, allow to simmer a further 10 minutes, uncovered. Drain, keeping fruit still moist. Cool, while preparing base.
❦ Preheat oven to moderate/180°C/375°F.
❦ To prepare base, cream butter and sugar together until light and fluffy. Beat in egg, fold in sifted flours. Spread mixture evenly over base of pan.
❦ Spoon fruits over base.
❦ To prepare topping, combine coconut, sugar or honey, rolled oats or crushed cornflakes, in a bowl, chop butter into tiny pieces, add. Spoon as evenly as possible over fruit.
❦ Bake for 10 minutes then reduce oven temperature to low/150°C/300°F. Cook a further 20–25 minutes, or until golden brown. Cool in tin 5 minutes.
❦ Serve warm with cream, or ice-cream.

SERVES 6

Water lily, Prospect Creek.

Apricots were first brought from China to Europe thence to Australia with the early settlers. They are a fragrant fruit with a high vitamin A content. Apricots can be eaten raw, poached, dried and preserved.

BOILED FRUIT CAKE

500 g/16 oz mixed dried fruit
250 g/8 oz butter
1 cup/250 ml/8 fl oz water
1 cup/250 g/8 oz sugar
1 teaspoon bicarbonate of soda
2 eggs, beaten
½ teaspoon almond essence
1 cup/125 g/4 oz plain flour
1 cup/125 g/4 oz self-raising flour
½ teaspoon each of nutmeg and cinnamon

❀ Preheat oven to slow/150°C/300°F.
❀ In a large pan, combine fruit, butter, water, sugar and bicarbonate of soda. Bring to boil and simmer 5 minutes. This mixture is likely to boil over, so watch carefully. Allow to cool. Cake will have a coarse texture if not allowed to cool before adding eggs and flour.
❀ Stir in eggs, one at a time, add almond essence. Sift together the flours and fold into the mixture. Spoon into a 20 cm/8 in cake pan, lined with 1 layer of foil and 1 layer of baking paper cut to fit pan with 2.5 cm/1 in overlapping the top of cake pan.
❀ Bake 1¾ hours or until cake is cooked when tested. Turn oven off and allow cake to cool in pan, in the oven. When cold, carefully lift cake out by holding onto the overlapping paper.
❀ Will keep for weeks in an airtight container.

> The Barossa Valley (meaning hill of roses) in South Australia, was named in 1837 by Colonel William Light. The area was first settled around 1840 by Lutherans escaping oppression in Silesia. The district has hot summers and regular winter rains which, combined with the rich soils, produce high quality wines and dried fruits.

Sunrise over beach.

SOUTH AUSTRALIA 45

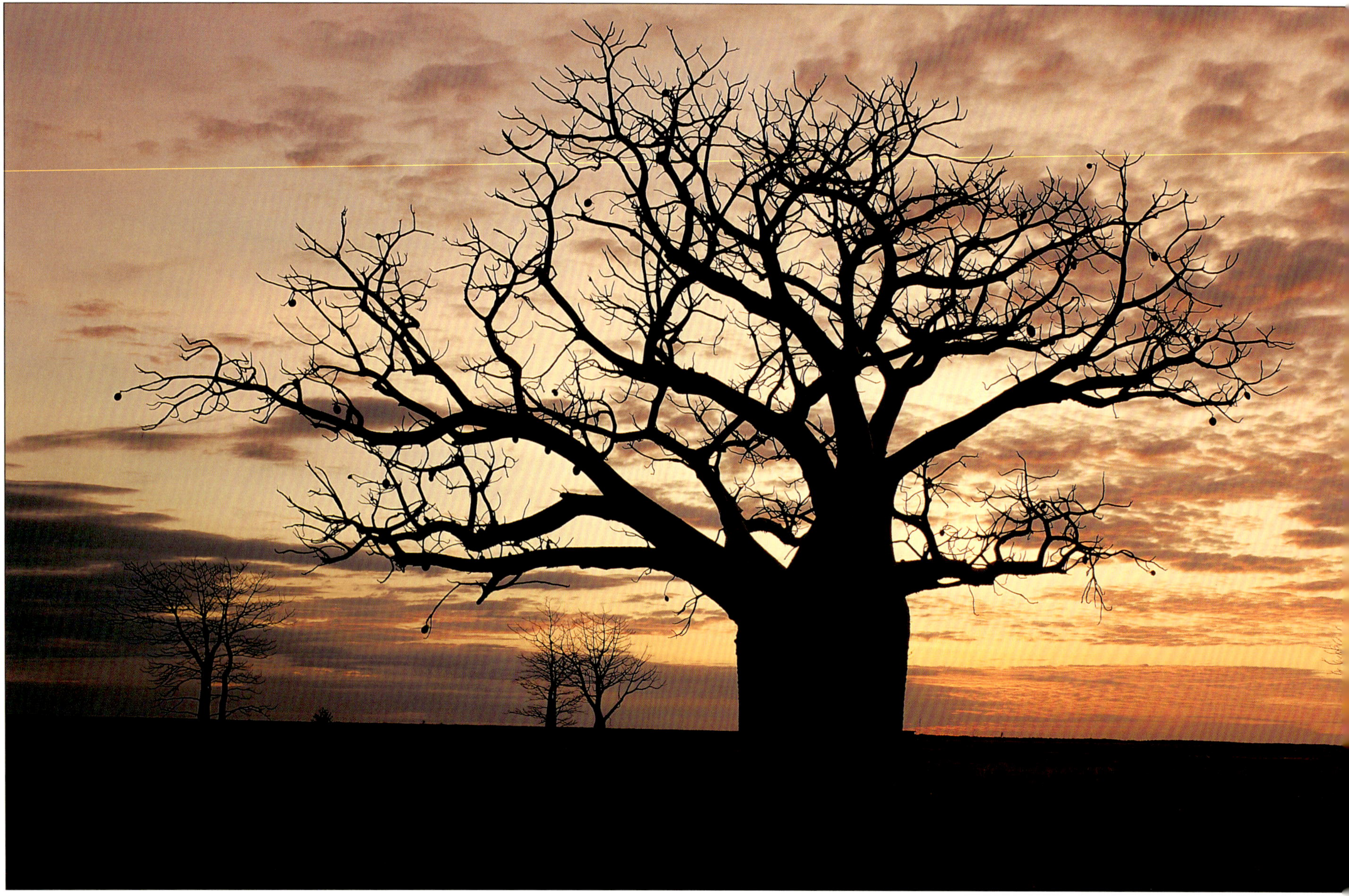

WESTERN AUSTRALIA

The Kimberley is the name given to the wilderness area in the north-west of this state. Cut off from the rest of the country on three sides by the ocean, the desert and the spectacular Bungle Bungle mountain range, many parts of the Kimberley are only accessible by helicopter or canoe.

This is the home of the magnificent pink diamond and also of many sacred hidden Aboriginal rock paintings. Mother Nature has blessed the Kimberley with waterfalls, unique rock formations, rare plants and animals, and extraordinary palms which sprout from the towering cliffs.

This is a place to stay a while so you can fully savour its natural, magical beauty and experience the taste of prawns in a quandong syrup or a hearty oxtail stew.

Boab Trees, WA.

Prawns Barbecued in Quandong (or apricot) Chilli Syrup

18 dried quandongs or dried apricot halves
1 cup water
juice 1 lemon
1/4 cup/60 ml/2 fl oz chilli sauce
1 1/2 tablespoons honey
4 green onions, finely chopped
2 tablespoons parsley, chopped
1/4 teaspoon Chinese five spice powder
18 large green prawns, with shells

❀ Cut the dried fruit in half. Combine all syrup ingredients together in a large pan. Marinate fruit and prawns, in their shells, in the syrup for 30 minutes.

❀ Remove prawns from syrup and bring the fruit and syrup to the boil, reduce heat and simmer 15 minutes.

❀ Preheat griller or barbecue. Soak 6 wooden skewers in cold water to prevent charring.

❀ Remove fruit from syrup and allow syrup to simmer until reduced by half. Remove from heat and return fruit to syrup.

❀ Thread 3 prawns per skewer. Wrap both ends of skewers in foil to prevent burning during cooking.

❀ Grill or barbecue skewers, turning once as the prawns turn pink. Brush both sides with the syrup when turning. Cook only until prawns turn light pink as overcooking toughens prawns.

❀ To serve, brush both sides of prawns with syrup before serving. Garnish with the quandong halves and a little syrup.

SERVES 6

West Beach, Esperance.

Quandongs are a native peach although they have a flavour closer to a tart apricot. They are used extensively by Aboriginal people as well as being made into preserves or being dried. The decorative seed can be crushed, then roasted for 5 minutes in an oven and nibbled with drinks.

Oxtail Stew

This stew is best cooked at least 24 hours before serving.

1 oxtail, cut into joints, trimmed of as much fat as possible
1 bay leaf
½ teaspoon dried thyme
1 300 g/10 oz can tomatoes
1 stick celery, diced
1 onion, diced
1 carrot, scraped and diced
1 zucchini, sliced into rounds
1 beef stock cube
3 potatoes, peeled and cut into 12 pieces
water

❀ Place oxtail in a large pan, add all ingredients (including juice from canned tomatoes) and sufficient water to just cover the meat. Cover and bring to boil, reduce heat and simmer until the meat is tender (this could take several hours). Allow stew to become cold so fat will solidify on the top of the stew. Remove as much of the fat as possible.
❀ Remove bay leaf.
❀ Serve hot with slices of bread and butter.

SERVES 3-4

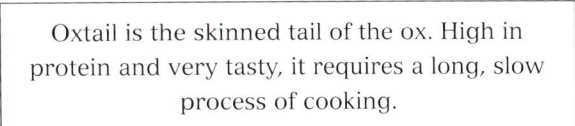

Oxtail is the skinned tail of the ox. High in protein and very tasty, it requires a long, slow process of cooking.

Palms, Echidna Chasm.

WESTERN AUSTRALIA 49

Kalumburu Road, Kimberley.

50 WESTERN AUSTRALIA

Dilly Bag Steak Filled with Chickpea Paste

PASTE

1 cup chickpeas

water

2 tablespoons oil

1 onion, finely diced

2 tablespoons pine nuts

1 medium size potato, cooked and dry mashed

1 clove garlic, crushed

BEEF

1 whole scotch fillet of beef

2 leaves silver beet, softened in hot water

1 tablespoon oil

2 teaspoons French mustard

juice of 1 lemon

salt and pepper

string for tying

❀ To prepare the paste, cover the chickpeas with water and soak overnight. Place the soaked chickpeas in a wide strainer in a large basin or sink of warm water. With the hands, pick up handfuls of the peas and rub between the palms, allowing the peas to drop back into the strainer. The skins will then lift away from the peas. Remove strainer from the water and if any skins are left on the peas, rub once more, and rinse.

❀ Heat oil and fry onions and pine nuts until lightly browned.

❀ Place peas in a blender or processor with browned onion and oil, nuts, potato and garlic. Blend or process until a thick paste is formed.

❀ Preheat oven to moderate/180°C/375°F.

❀ To prepare the beef, open out the fillet. Cut silver beet into strips and line the opened fillet. Fill the centre of the beef with the paste. Re-wrap the fillet tightly and secure with string. Combine remaining ingredients and brush the fillet all over. Place on a rack in a baking dish and cook for 30 minutes.

❀ To serve, remove string, cut fillet into thick slices and serve with cooked baby carrots, snap peas and whole new potatoes.

SERVES 6

Note: Dilly bag is the name given to the woven grass bag the Aboriginal women carried when searching for roots and berries.

The building of a diversion dam at Lake Kununurra has resulted in the growing of many tropical crops which are transported to the markets thousands of miles away. Included in these crops are chickpeas, noted for their high protein and fibre content.

WHOLE SNAPPER WITH TUNA MOUSSELINE

MOUSSELINE
1 small can tuna (approximately 105 g/3-4 oz)
1 egg white, stiffly whipped
2 tablespoons thick cream
1 tablespoon chopped fresh dill, or 2 teaspoons dried thyme
juice of ½ lemon
½ red capsicum, diced

SNAPPER
1 whole snapper, cleaned and scaled
juice of ½ lemon
½ cup/125 ml/4 fl oz white wine
large spinach leaf, capsicum strips and lemon slice to garnish

❦ To prepare mousseline, drain tuna and mash with a fork. Combine all mousseline ingredients.
❦ Preheat oven to moderate/180°C/375°F.
❦ To prepare fish, fill cavity of the snapper with the mousseline, secure with toothpicks. Place fish in a greased baking dish. Combine lemon juice and wine, and pour over the fish. Cover with greased foil. Bake 20–30 minutes until fish is tender.
❦ Carefully remove from baking dish, remove toothpicks.
❦ Rinse spinach leaf in hot water to wilt, drain.
❦ To serve, place spinach leaf on a platter. Carefully lay snapper on top and garnish with capsicum and lemon.

SERVES 2-4 depending on size of snapper

Aboriginal painting.

Snapper is a saltwater fish. Known as 'cockney bream' when young, then 'red bream', 'squire' and 'old man' as it increases in age. Snapper is sometimes referred to as 'queen fish' in Western Australia and 'red emperor' in Queensland but whatever its name, it is a delicious white fleshed fish.

OUR OWN PAVLOVA

A dessert that is crisp on the outside, marshmallow on the inside. This pavlova, unfilled, will keep for a week in an airtight container.

6 eggs, separated
2 cups/440 g/14 oz caster sugar
2 teaspoons cornflour
2 teaspoons white vinegar
2 teaspoons cold water
1 teaspoon vanilla essence
300 ml/10 fl oz cream, whipped thickly
4 passionfruit

❃ Preheat oven to moderate/180°C/375°F.
❃ Whisk egg whites until very stiff, gradually add the sugar, a spoonful at a time, beating well until sugar dissolves. With a fork or whisk, add cornflour, vinegar, water and vanilla.
❃ Run a greased flat oven tray or pavlova plate under cold water leaving small beads of water on the plate. Pile the mixture into the centre and make a small indentation in the centre of the pavlova.
❃ Bake on lowest shelf of oven for 15 minutes.
❃ Turn oven temperature down to low/150°C/300°F and bake for a further 10 minutes.
❃ Turn oven OFF, without opening the door, and leave for 2 hours.
❃ To serve, pile the centre of the pavlova with whipped cream and top with passionfruit pulp.

SERVES 6-8

> Pavlova was created by the chef, Herbert Sachse in 1935 and was named by Harry Nairne from the Esplanade Hotel, Perth, after the visiting Russian ballerina, Pavlova. It is said the built up sides of the dessert reminded him of a tutu.

Salmon gums, Goomalling.

Overleaf: *Bell Creek Falls, Kimberley.*

WESTERN AUSTRALIA 53

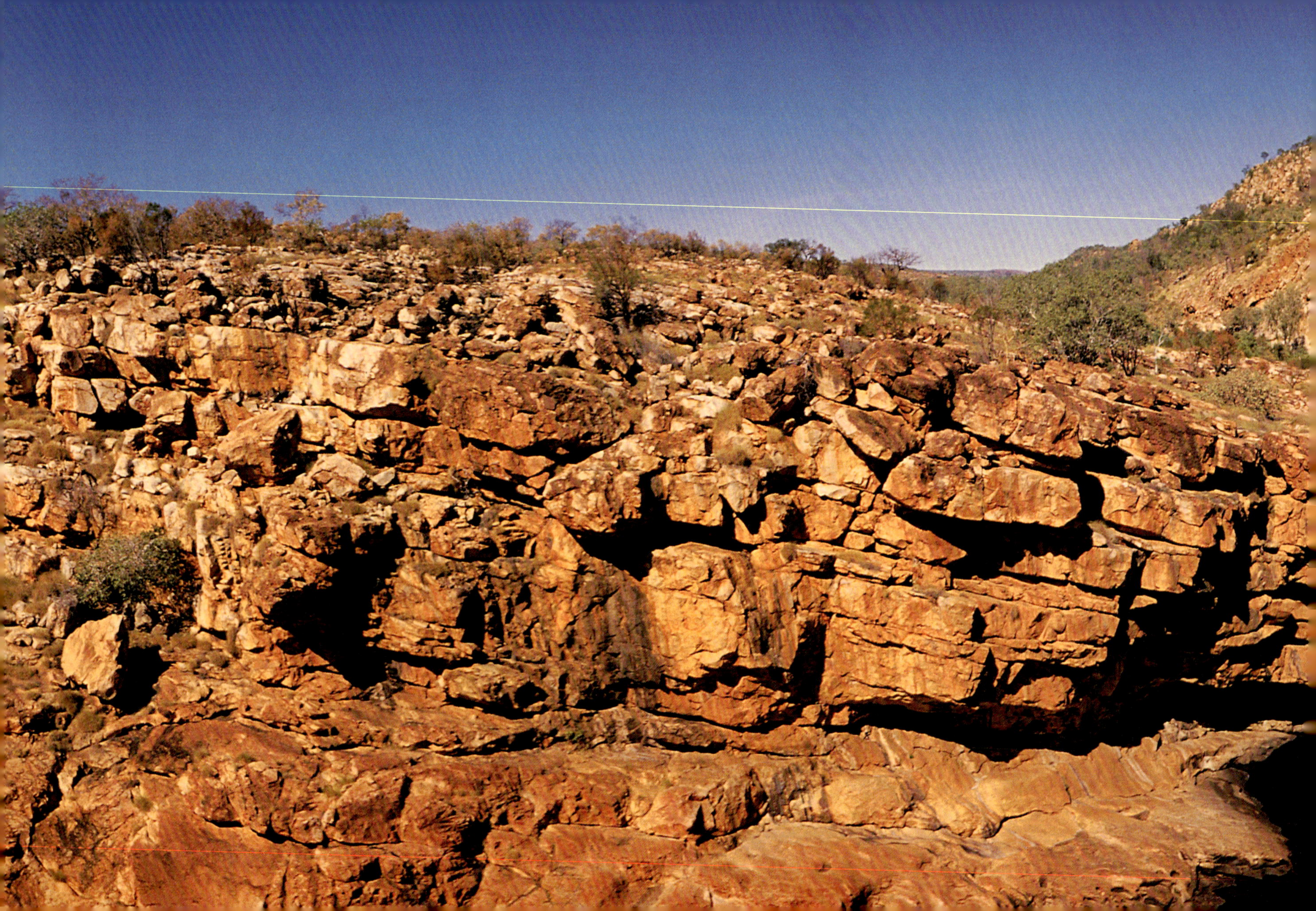

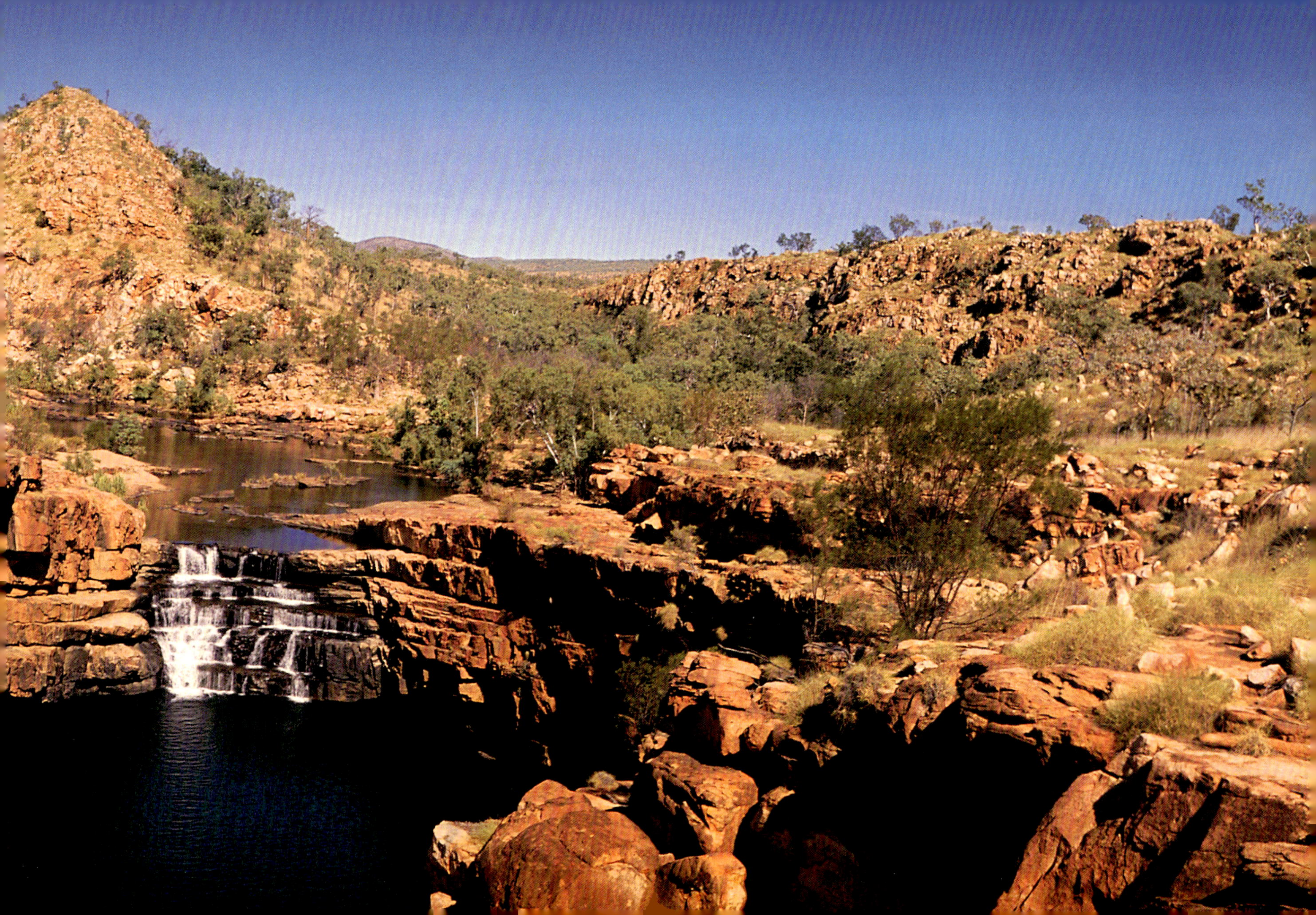

BREAD AND BUTTER PUDDING

6 slices white bread, crusts removed
butter
2 tablespoons each of currants and sultanas
2 eggs
1 tablespoon caster sugar
1¾ cups/430 ml/14 fl oz milk, warmed

TOPPING
1 tablespoon caster sugar
½ teaspoon dried nutmeg
1 tablespoon desiccated coconut

❦ Preheat oven to moderate/180°C/375°F.
❦ To prepare pudding, cut bread into small squares and butter lightly. Line the base of a greased, shallow dish, with ½ of the bread squares, butter side up. Sprinkle with the mixed fruit. Cover the mixed fruit with the remaining bread squares, buttered side down. Beat together the eggs, sugar and warmed milk and carefully pour over the mixture in the dish.
❦ To prepare topping, combine the ingredients and sprinkle over the mixture. Place dish in a baking dish with a little water in the base (this prevents the custard boiling and curdling). Bake 30–40 minutes until the mixture has set.
❦ Serve hot or cold.

SERVES 6

Ant hill, Bungle Bungles.

> This is one of the recipes brought out by the early settlers and adopted as a firm favourite. Until the latter half of this century bread was delivered daily by horse and cart. The baker not only brought bread but the much coveted manure dropped by the horse. Whichever household was fortunate enough to have this steaming pile dropped at its gate, immediately scooped up the fertiliser to spread on the garden.

ANZAC Biscuits

These biscuits will keep for a week in an airtight container.

1 cup/90 g/3 oz rolled oats
1 cup/125 g/4 oz self-raising flour
1 cup/220 g/7 oz caster sugar
1 cup/90 g/3 oz desiccated coconut
1 tablespoon golden syrup
125 g/4 oz butter
½ teaspoon bicarbonate soda
1 tablespoon boiling water

❀ Preheat oven to moderate/180°C/375°F.
❀ Mix dry ingredients together. Melt butter and golden syrup and pour into dry ingredients. Combine bicarbonate with water, stir into mixture. Drop spoonfuls of mixture onto a greased scone tray. Press down with a fork to flatten. Bake 10–15 minutes until brown. Cool.

MAKES APPROXIMATELY 48

The Australian and New Zealand Army Corps joined together to fight in the First World War. The abbreviation of this name 'A.N.Z.A.C.' was stamped onto boxes awaiting shipment. When a code name was required, the name ANZAC was adopted. The term usually applies to those who served at Gallipoli. Each year, the 25th April is set aside as a Remembrance Day, with marches and wreath laying ceremonies throughout Australia.

Wattle tree.

WESTERN AUSTRALIA 57

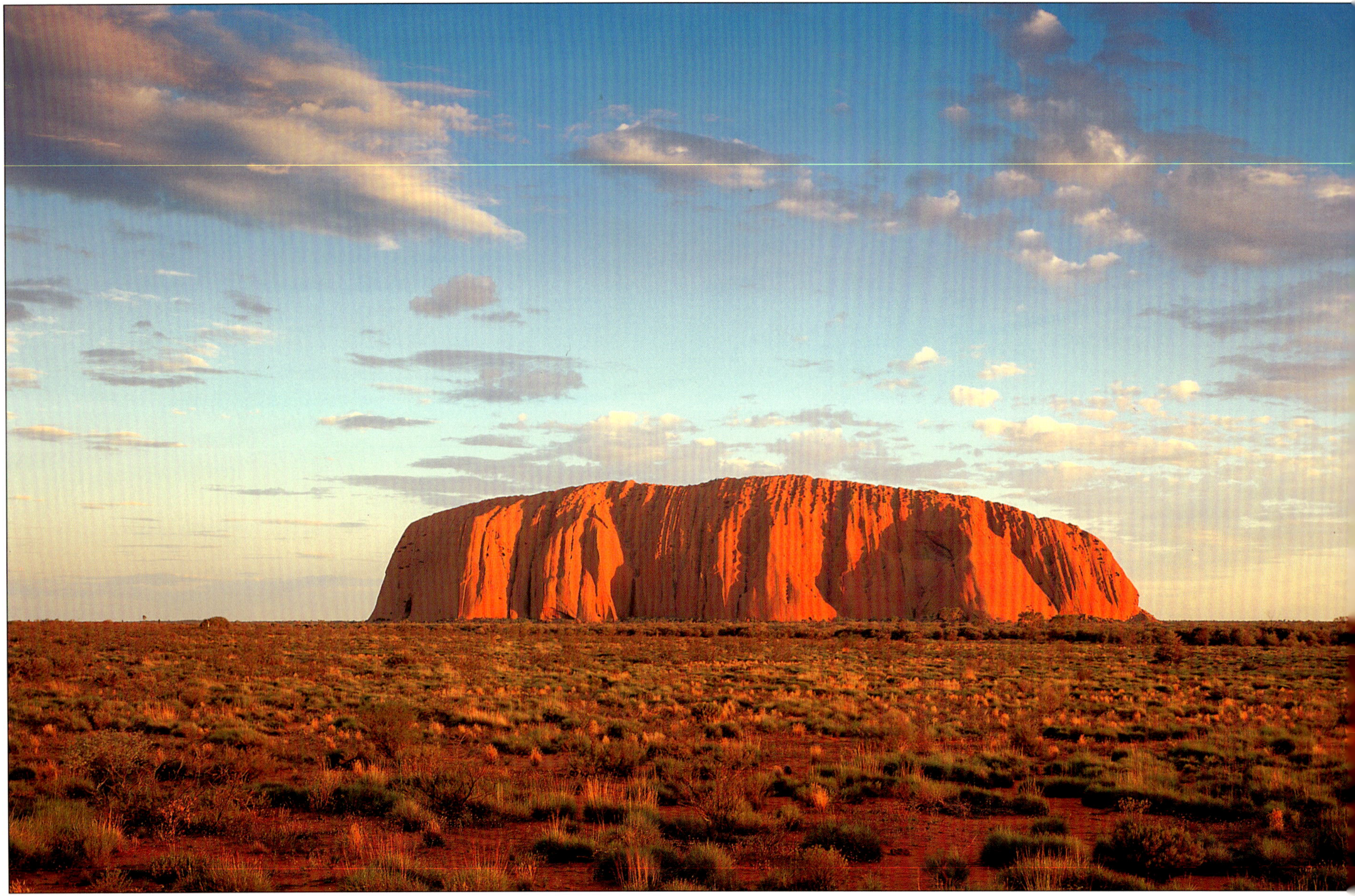

Northern Territory

Uluru is the traditional Aboriginal name for one of the world's most extraordinary and beautiful rock formations. As the dawn breaks, watch the fascinating play of light and shade on Uluru as it seems to rise from the stark flat landscape around it. Feast on a lavish breakfast with all the trimmings including damper—a food famous throughout Australia and one that truly reflects a part of our history.

The Northern Territory is a land of stark contrasts and one that is rich in Australian Aboriginal heritage and culture. Dusty red dirt roads weave from dry wind-blown deserts to dramatic sheer rock-walled gorges.

It is also an area that produces some unusual and adventurous foods—try crocodile in beer batter or our famous barramundi.

Timeless Land, Uluru, NT.

Eggs in a Hole

1 thick slice bread
1 tablespoon dripping or butter
1 egg

❦ Cut the centre from the bread. Heat dripping in a pan and fry bread on one side until lightly golden in colour. Carefully turn bread over and break the egg into the hole. Continue cooking until egg is set. Gently remove egg and bread from pan with a spatula.
❦ Serve immediately, for breakfast, perhaps with grilled sausages and tomatoes.

SERVES 1

Damper Dripping with Golden Syrup

3 cups/375 g/12 oz self-raising flour
1 teaspoon salt
90 g/3 oz butter
½ cup/125 ml/4 fl oz milk
½ cup/125 ml/4 fl oz cold water
extra flour for kneading
1 tablespoon milk, extra
1 tablespoon plain flour, extra
golden syrup, to serve

❦ Preheat oven to hot/250°C/475°F.
❦ Sift flour and salt into a bowl. Rub in butter with fingertips until mixture resembles fine sand. Make a well in the centre and cut in liquids with a knife until it forms a soft ball. Turn mixture out onto a floured sheet and knead until a smooth dough. Pat into a round shape approximately 15 cm/6 in, in diameter. Place on a greased oven tray, brush with extra milk and sprinkle top with 1 tablespoon flour.
❦ Bake 25–30 minutes.
❦ Serve hot, cut into rounds with heaps of golden syrup and a mug of Billy tea.

❦ Damper is an Australian version of bread. Golden syrup is a treacle made from the evaporation of the sugar cane juice and is also known as 'Cocky's Joy'

Damper was usually cooked in a camp oven and always served with tea. The name 'Billy tea' originated in the gold rush times when French Boeuf (beef), was imported in tins. The miners or 'diggers' mispronounced boeuf to 'bully' then 'billy'. The empty tins were used to boil water to make tea.

Seared Buffalo Fillet with Goat Cheese Balls

MARINADE

1 cup/250 ml/8 fl oz red wine
½ teaspoon dried thyme and basil
1 teaspoon French mustard
1 tablespoon oil
fillet of buffalo cut into thin steaks
butter or oil
mixed lettuce leaves, to garnish

❀ Combine all of the marinade ingredients and marinate steaks for 30 minutes to 1 hour.
❀ Heat barbecue or melt butter/oil in a skillet.
❀ Remove fillet steaks from marinade and sear for 45 seconds on both sides.
❀ To serve, arrange mixed leaves on a plate, place slices of fillet on top and drizzle a little warmed marinade over the steaks. Serve with small balls of goat cheese.

SERVES 6-8

GOAT CHEESE BALLS

60 g/2 oz goat's cheese
½ teaspoon coriander seeds, crushed
1 tablespoon light sour cream

❀ Cream the cheese with coriander and sour cream, chill. Form cheese into balls.

Bullocks were introduced to the colony in 1795 and were essential in hauling timber, wool, etc. In 1820 the buffalo were domesticated but when settlements were abandoned they became feral. A factory was established in Darwin for the production of ghee (butter made from buffalo milk) in 1886. Buffalo meat is now exported and is slowly being accepted into our cuisine.

God's Marbles, Tennant Creek.

NORTHERN TERRITORY 61

Kata Tjuta.

Barramundi with Orange Sauce and Warm Salad

2 barramundi fillets
squeeze lemon juice
oil

❀ Preheat oven to moderate/180°C/375°F or heat the barbecue.
❀ Place fillets on a greased piece of foil, squeeze lemon juice over the fillets and brush with a little oil. Wrap foil over fish to make a parcel.
❀ Bake or barbecue for approximately 10–15 minutes or until tender.
❀ To serve, carefully lift onto plates and spoon a little of the juices over the fillets. Serve with a Warm Salad and an Orange or Mango Sauce (see Lamb in Macadamia Crust recipe).

SERVES 2

Warm Salad

½ carrot, scraped
1 stick celery
1 green onion, white and green parts
½ red capsicum, seeded
1 zucchini
1 teaspoon oil
3 drops sesame oil

❀ Finely shred all vegetables. Heat oil in a pan and fry vegetables 30 seconds. Sprinkle with sesame oil. Serve whilst warm.

Orange Sauce

20 g/½ oz butter
1 green onion, white part, finely diced
½ cup/125 ml/4 fl oz orange juice
40 g/1½ oz butter, extra

❀ Heat butter and fry green onion for 1 minute. Stir in orange juice, bring to boil. Remove from heat. Beat in extra butter a little at a time.
❀ To serve, place fillets on plates, spoon over sauce and serve with a warm salad and a few orange segments.

Palm fronds, Mataranka.

NORTHERN TERRITORY 63

Crocodile in Beer Batter with Curry Mayonnaise

250 g/8 oz crocodile meat cut into 1 cm/½ in strips

MARINADE

1 cup/250 ml/8 fl oz white wine
2 teaspoons ground turmeric
2 teaspoons sugar
1 tablespoon soy sauce
1 teaspoon ground coriander
½ teaspoon ground cumin
1 teaspoon garam masala
1 clove garlic, crushed

BEER BATTER

1 cup/125 g/4 oz plain flour
pinch salt
½ cup beer
cold water
oil or fat, for deep frying

❊ To prepare the marinade, combine all marinade ingredients. Totally cover crocodile pieces with marinade and allow to stand at least 2 hours or longer, turning occasionally.

❊ To prepare the batter, combine flour, salt and beer in a bowl, add sufficient cold water to make the batter into a thick liquid. Heat the oil/fat. Remove the crocodile from the marinade and dip into the thick batter. Fry the pieces in the heated oil/fat until golden brown. Drain. Repeat until all the crocodile is cooked.

❊ Serve while hot. Place the curry mayonnaise in a small dish and dip the crocodile pieces into the mayonnaise.

SERVES 6

Note: A coarse fleshed fish or chicken may be substituted for the crocodile in this recipe if desired.

Curry Mayonnaise

1 cup prepared mayonnaise
2 teaspoons curry powder

❊ Mix the mayonnaise and curry powder together until smooth.

There are two types of crocodile found in Australia: freshwater or estuarine, and saltwater. The latter is the largest. Males reach an average length of 5 metres, although some have been recorded at 8 metres.
The estuarine crocodile is mainly responsible for human deaths. The crocodile stalks its victim over a period of days before attacking. If the attack is successful the crocodile drags its victim to a water 'kitchen' and allows it to soften before eating. The crocodile has been a protected species since 1972. It is now commercially farmed for eating.

Kings Canyon.

BLACK BARRAMUNDI

2 barramundi fillets
½ teaspoon each of dried oregano and thyme
1 teaspoon freshly ground black pepper
1 teaspoon white pepper
1 teaspoon garlic powder
4 teaspoons sweet paprika
1 teaspoon onion salt

❦ Preheat oven to moderate/180°C/375°F or heat the barbecue.

❦ Combine all spices and push through a fine strainer. Thickly coat the top of the fillet with the spice mixture. Sear on barbecue or in a greased pan on top of the stove until blackened. Continue cooking on barbecue a further 8–10 minutes or finish in the oven for 8–10 minutes.

❦ To serve, place fillets on a plate and serve with a Warm Salad and Orange Sauce (recipes page 63) or Lemon Saffron Sauce. To make Lemon Saffron Sauce, follow the Orange Sauce recipe and substitute lemon juice and ½ teaspoon saffron powder for the orange juice.

SERVES 1-2

Note: This is a very spicy, slightly dry way of cooking the barramundi.

Barramundi is the Aboriginal name for this very large, fresh water fish. Smaller, plate size barramundi are now being cultivated in fish farms in the Northern Territory.

A favourite at all barbecues are potatoes baked in coals. When the fire has died down leaving glowing coals, a potato with the skin pricked once, is buried amongst the coals and allowed to cook there for about 45 minutes. When pulled out, the skin is deeply charcoaled. The top is cut off and a spoon is used to loosen the flesh. A knob of butter is forced into the flesh which is then eaten from the blackened skin. This must be the best tasting potato in the world.

Sturt's Desert Pea.

Pawpaw Mousse Wrapped in Spun Sugar

500 g/16 oz pawpaw, peeled and seeded
¼ cup/60 ml/2 fl oz Grand Marnier or Kirsch liqueur
¼ cup/60 g/2 oz caster sugar
300 ml/10 fl oz cream, whipped until thick
4 egg whites, stiffly whipped

❋ Puree the pawpaw in a blender or processor or push through a sieve with liqueur until liquidised. Chill 20 minutes. Stir the sugar into whipped cream, stir into puree. Fold whipped egg whites into the mixture.

❋ Pile into glass dishes and chill until ready to serve.

Spun Sugar

½ cup/110 g/3½ oz caster sugar
2 tablespoons water

❋ When ready to serve the mousse, place sugar and water in a small pan, stir over heat until sugar dissolves. Allow to simmer until the mixture just starts to turn golden then remove immediately from heat. Dip a fork into the mixture and as you lift it up out of the pan pull the mixture into fine strands with your fingers and swirl over the mousse. Repeat until each mousse is topped with sugar.

SERVES 6

Pawpaw or papaya originally came from tropical America. The yellow fruit contains many small black seeds which, if eaten, give the tongue a 'pins and needles' feel, but they are sometimes used as a spice. The enzyme, papain, which is found in the pawpaw, is used as a meat tenderiser, in chewing gum, and as a medicine. It is reputed, that if pawpaw is eaten regularly, it has soothing properties for back troubles.

Sunset on Lake Boomanjin.

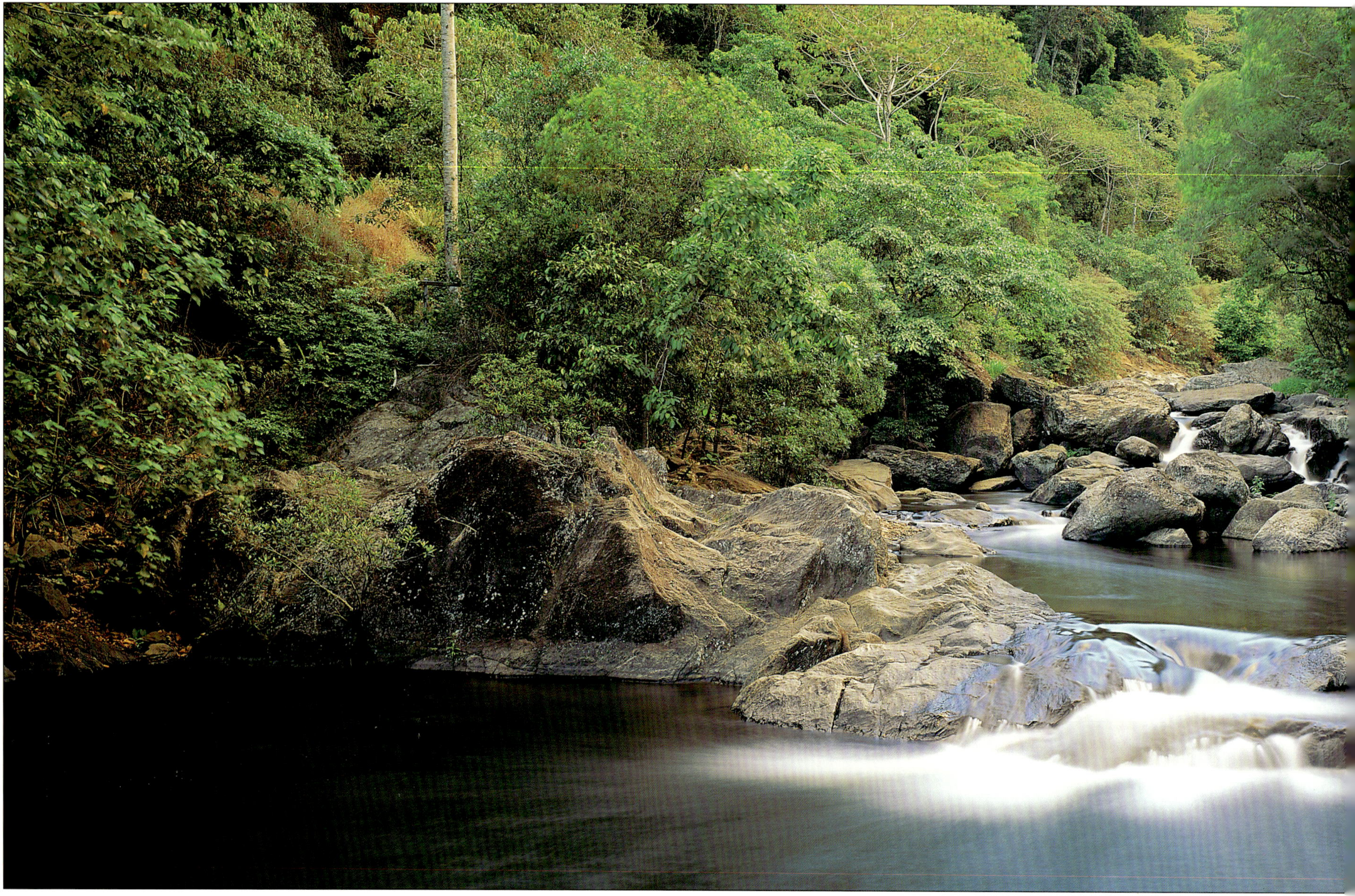

Queensland

This state is home to the Great Barrier Reef, the world's largest underwater coral garden and home to countless jewel-coloured fish.

Queensland is best known as a tropical paradise of rivers, waterfalls, lakes, beaches and islands. However, this home to World Heritage-listed areas is, like most states in Australia, a land of great contrast, from Fraser Island, the world's largest sand island, to the rich green rainforest of the Daintree National Park or the vast, remote and thinly populated Gulf Country.

In sunny Queensland, the food is as varied and lavish as the landscape, ranging from the spectacular seafood and tropical fruits of the lush coastal regions through to traditional homestead favourites, such as lamingtons and pumpkin scones.

Crystal Cascades, Cairns, QLD.

Chicken Kebabs in Peanut Sauce

juice of 1 lemon
4 chicken fillets or 125 g/4 oz chicken tenderloins cut into cubes
2 tablespoons oil
1 cup rice
½ teaspoon saffron
hot water
peanut sauce and green onion curls, to garnish

❀ Preheat griller or barbecue.
❀ Squeeze lemon juice over chicken. Thread onto 12 wooden skewers that have been soaked in water to prevent charring. Place a sheet of foil on a griller or barbecue and cover wooden ends of skewers with a sheet of foil to protect ends from burning. Cook skewers 4 minutes, turn, brush with a little more lemon juice and oil. Cook a further 4 minutes.
❀ Cover rice and saffron with hot water. Bring to boil and allow to simmer until all water has been absorbed. Saffron is used to delicately flavour and colour the rice yellow.
❀ If you prefer to use a microwave, cover rice and saffron with hot water, cover dish. Cook on HIGH 10–15 minutes, until all water has been absorbed.
❀ To serve, place saffron rice on a serving plate with kebabs and green onion curls, pour sauce over the kebabs.
SERVES 4 (3-4 kebabs per serve)

Peanut Sauce

1 tablespoon oil
1 onion, peeled and grated
½ cup/125 ml/4 fl oz extra oil
150 g/5 oz peanuts, shelled, with ½ tablespoon cornflour or 1 cup peanut butter
1 teaspoon chopped chillies
2 cloves garlic, crushed
½ cup/125 ml/4 fl oz water
1 tablespoon soy sauce
juice of 1 lemon
1 teaspoon sugar

❀ Heat 1 tablespoon of oil, gently fry onion until soft and transparent.
❀ If you prefer to use a microwave, place 1 tablespoon oil and onion in a dish, cook on HIGH 2 minutes.
❀ Combine all ingredients and process or put through blender until smooth. Return to pan and stir until mixture boils and thickens.
❀ To finish in microwave, return to dish, heat on HIGH 2 minutes, stir.

Note: When handling chillies avoid touching your face, particularly the eyes, as chilli contains a volatile oil which burns.

Green Onion Curls

1 green onion
bowl chilled water

❀ Cut green onion into 2.5 cm/1 in lengths. With scissors, cut both ends four times toward the centre, just leaving a small uncut centre. Place in chilled water until the ends curl.

> Peanuts were first grown in the Kingaroy area around 1900 from seeds obtained from the Chinese who came to the Nanango area seeking gold. By 1928 the first silo was built and by 1990 nearly 60 000 tonne of peanuts were being handled

Pillows of Moreton Bay Bugs with Tomato Relish

6 Moreton Bay bugs, cooked
20 g/½ oz butter
1 green onion, white and green sections, diced
1 tablespoon plain flour
2 teaspoons brandy
½ cup/125 ml/4 fl oz cream or milk
commercial spring roll pastry
extra flour
1 egg yolk mixed with milk, to glaze
oil/fat for deep frying

❦ Remove bug meat from shells, cut the bug meat into small pieces. Melt butter and lightly fry green onion for 30 seconds. Add flour, stirring until the flour begins to bubble, remove from heat and beat in brandy and milk. Return to heat and stir until mixture boils and thickens. Remove from heat and add bug meat. Cool.

❦ Lay the spring roll sheets on a sheet of paper dusted with flour. Cut the spring roll sheets into 4. Place a teaspoon of bug mixture in centre of each square of pastry, brush edges with egg and milk mixture, fold over, forming a triangle and press firmly together. Chill for 10 minutes.

❦ Heat oil/fat for deep frying. Fry pillows until they are a pale brown colour. Drain, keep hot.

❦ To serve, place a spoonful of relish on a serving plate with pillows.

MAKES 16, depending on size

Tomato Relish

1 tablespoon oil
1 onion, sliced
1 x 500 g/16 oz can tomatoes
½ celery stalk, diced
½ green capsicum, sliced
1 bay leaf
6 peppercorns
½ teaspoon dried thyme
6 fresh basil leaves, or 1 teaspoon dried basil
1 teaspoon sugar

❦ Heat oil and gently fry onion, celery and capsicum until onion is transparent. Add remaining ingredients including juice from tomatoes. Bring to boil and simmer uncovered for 5 minutes, mashing the tomatoes as they cook. Remove bay leaf and peppercorns (if the relish is too thin, thicken with a little cornflour paste).

> The Moreton Bay area is rich in seafood. Historical documents note that Aboriginals in this area trained dolphins to herd schools of fish to the shore where they were speared. The dolphin was thought to be a protector of dead spirits.

Hill Inlet, Whitsunday Island.

QUEENSLAND 71

Hardys Reef, Great Barrier Reef.

FLAMBE OF TROPICAL FRUITS

1 pineapple, cut in half lengthwise through green top
12 strawberries, whole with green tips
1 banana, peeled, sliced diagonally
2 mandarins, peeled, in segments with skin removed
1 tablespoon brandy or rum, in a small dish
1 tablespoon brown sugar, in a small dish
1 tablespoon whipped cream, in a small dish, sprinkled with brown sugar
3 sugar cubes, in a small dish
1 teaspoon lemon essence

❦ Place the two halves of the pineapple on a large serving dish. With a sharp knife cube and remove all flesh. Pile the cubed pineapple in ¼ of pineapple shell, next place strawberries, then mandarin segments, finally sliced banana.

❦ Arrange the 4 dishes in front of the filled pineapple and pour lemon essence over sugar cubes and set them alight.

❦ Using a fondue fork, dip pieces of fruit into rum or brandy, roll in brown sugar, then hold over flame to caramelise. Dip into cream and pop into mouth.

SERVES 2-3

> Rum played a very important part in the early colony of New South Wales. Because of a shortage in coins and luxury goods, rum was used for barter to buy both labour and food. In 1808 Governor William Bligh (of *Mutiny on the Bounty* fame), tried to prohibit the making and trafficking of rum and a rebellion known as the 'Rum Rebellion', led by the army corp, broke out. It was not until 1816–17, with the foundation of the Bank of New South Wales, that silver coinage was established and the rum trade diminished. Today the best rum is manufactured at Bundaberg, Queensland.

Fan palms, Daintree National Park.

Pumpkin Scones Smothered with Butter

Jap or butternut pumpkins are most suitable for cake and dessert making.

60 g/2 oz butter
¼ cup/60 g/2 oz caster sugar
½ cup pumpkin, cooked, dry mashed (approximately 200g/6½ oz pumpkin with skin will yield ½ cup cooked pumpkin)
1 egg
2 tablespoons cold milk
2½ cups/300 g/10 oz self-raising flour
pinch salt
extra flour
extra milk, for glazing
butter, to serve

❀ Preheat oven to moderate/180°C/375°F.
❀ Cream butter and sugar together, stir in pumpkin. Stir in egg and half the milk. Sift flour and salt together and fold into mixture with remainder of milk. Turn out onto a floured sheet and knead into a smooth ball, approximately 3.5 cm/1½ in thick.
❀ Cut into rounds and place on tray. Glaze with a little milk and bake, 15–20 minutes.
❀ Serve hot, split in half with heaps of butter.

MAKES 12-14

Pumpkin Soup

500 g/16 oz butternut pumpkin
20 g/½ oz butter
1 onion, sliced
1 small potato, peeled
3 cups water
2 chicken stock cubes, crumbled
light sour cream and 1 tablespoon snipped chives, to garnish

❀ Peel pumpkin and cut into pieces. Heat butter in a deep pan and gently fry onion until transparent. Add pumpkin, potato, water and stock cubes, bring to boil and simmer 45 minutes until pumpkin is very soft. Cool slightly and blend.
❀ To serve, ladle soup into bowls, swirl a little cream on the top and sprinkle with chopped chives.

SERVES 4-6

> Pumpkin is a member of the 'gourd' family, also known as squash in some countries. There are many varieties of pumpkin ranging from tiny green and yellow striped to brilliant orange skinned to smooth grey and knobbly pale brown. They are used as decorations, candle holders and of course the famous 'jack-o'-lantern'.

Mud Crab with Coconut Sauce

1 mud crab, cooked
2 teaspoons oil
1 small onion, finely diced
60 g/2 oz coconut milk
1 teaspoon crushed garlic
½ teaspoon sugar
squeeze lemon juice
½ teaspoon each of cumin, coriander
½ cup/125 ml/4 fl oz natural yoghurt
1 tablespoon shredded coconut
green onion curls to garnish (see Chicken Kebabs recipe)

❧ Carefully cut crab shell in half. Remove meat from shell and shred. Rinse shell and replace the shredded meat in the bottom half of the shell. Top with other half of shell so it looks like the crab is whole.

❧ Heat oil and lightly fry onion, add coconut milk, garlic, sugar, lemon juice, spices and yoghurt and stir until hot but do not boil. Either spoon into half a fresh coconut shell or into a small bowl for dipping.

❧ Toast the shredded coconut in a pan, stirring until golden brown. If you prefer to use a microwave for this step, place coconut in a bowl cook on HIGH 30 seconds, stir, cook a further 30 seconds or until brown.

❧ Toss toasted coconut on top of dressing.

❧ To serve, arrange crab on a serving plate with bowl of dressing and garnish with green onion curls. Have a small finger bowl of warm water with a slice of lemon plus a small towel, and claw crackers on the table.

SERVES 1

Note: The addition of ½ cup tomato paste and ½-1 teaspoon crushed chilli to the coconut sauce makes a delightful sauce to serve hot with the crab.

Golden shower, Lake Moondarra.

Coconuts are not native Australian fruit. The trees were planted in North Queensland by early seamen visiting the shores to provide food for shipwrecked sailors. All of the coconut is useable. The milk is refreshing and nourishing, the flesh is edible and nutritious, while the fibre can be woven into baskets and hats. Most of the flesh from the coconut is dried to form copra from which coconut oil is extracted.

Rich Farmland, Glasshouse Mountains.

76 QUEENSLAND

Lamingtons

The cake is best made the day before and thoroughly chilled or frozen, before icing. Lamingtons freeze very well for up to six months.

Cake

3 large eggs
½ cup/110 g/3½ oz caster sugar
¾ cup/95 g/3 oz self-raising flour
¼ cup/30 g/1 oz cornflour
10 g/⅓ oz butter
3 tablespoons hot milk

❈ Preheat oven to moderate/180°C/375°F.
❈ Beat eggs until thick and light, gradually add the sugar, beating well until sugar has dissolved. Sift dry ingredients together, fold into egg mixture.
❈ Dissolve butter in milk and fold into cake mixture. Spoon into a greased 18 cm x 28 cm/7 in x 11 in lamington tin and bake 25–30 minutes. Turn out onto cake cooler. Chill or freeze overnight.
❈ Cut into 16 pieces.

Chocolate Icing

500 g/16 oz icing sugar
½ cup/50 g/2 oz cocoa
10 g/⅓ oz butter
½ cup/125 ml/4 fl oz warmed milk
3 cups/250 g/8 oz desiccated coconut

❈ Sift icing sugar with cocoa into a bowl. Melt butter in milk and pour into icing mixture, stir well. Stand bowl in hot water while coating cake.
❈ Place coconut in a plastic bag.
❈ With a fork or tongs, dip one portion of cake into chocolate icing, shake gently and carefully place in plastic bag. Shake bag to coat cake in coconut, lift out and stand on cake cooler to dry.
❈ Repeat. If icing begins to thicken, add a little hot water to make a thick liquid.

MAKES 16

Spinafex fires.

Lamingtons were named after Lord Lamington, Governor of Queensland between 1895-1901. Because of the heat in Queensland, cakes left out of storage tins would quickly dry out. Rather than throw the cake away, or give it to the dogs, a resourceful cook covered the cake in chocolate icing and coconut, thus making the cake moist once more.

QUEENSLAND

GLOSSARY and Substitutes ((s) for substitutions)

barramundi (s) white, large flaked fish
bicarbonate of soda (s) baking soda
buffalo (s) fillet beef
butter (s) margarine
capsicum bell pepper
chickpeas garbanzos
chilli sauce commercial sauce made from chillies, sugar, garlic, vinegar
coconut, desiccated (s) shredded coconut
cornflour cornstarch
crayfish large cray or lobster
cream fresh pouring cream
cream, sour commercially cultured soured cream
crocodile (s) coarse flesh fish, alligator
crushed minced, pressed, fresh or commercial
dripping beef fat or lard
English spinach (s) young silver beet
fat blended animal, vegetable oil, solidified
flour, plain all purpose flour
ginger fresh, commercially crushed
golden syrup (s) maple syrup, treacle, honey
grease thin layer of butter or oil
greaseproof, baking paper wax proof paper
green apples cooking apples, firm flesh
green onions shallots, scallions, spring onions
grill broil

horseradish cream or crushed
kangaroo available overseas (s) beef
lavender honey (s) honey
macadamia (s) hazelnuts
mince ground beef
mud crabs (s) crabs
oil, for dressings first pressed virgin olive oil
oil, for frying polyunsaturated vegetable oil
pan skillet, pot
pawpaw papaya
plastic wrap cling film
prawns shrimps
pumpkin (s) canned pumpkin or orange squash
quandong (s) small apricots
snapper soft pink/white fleshed fish
snow peas mange-tout, cooked in their pods
stock cubes bouillon cubes
sugar, brown soft, moist, finely grained, brown colour
sugar, caster superfine sugar
sugar peas snap peas (mange-tout), cooked in their pods
sugar icing confectioner's, powdered sugar
sultanas seedless white raisins
tomato sauce tomato ketchup
wattle seed (s) ground hazelnuts
yabbies fresh water crayfish

WEIGHTS AND MEASURES GUIDE

MEASUREMENT GUIDE
Australian
cup measurement = 250 ml
spoon measurement 1 tablespoon = 20 ml
1 teaspoon = 5 ml
Some overseas countries
1 tablespoon = 15 ml (in most recipes there will not be a notable difference, however, an extra 1 teaspoon may be added)
1 teaspoon = 0.2 fl oz

DRY MEASUREMENTS

Metric	Imperial
125 g	4 oz (¼ lb)
250 g	8 oz (½ lb)
375 g	12 oz (¾ lb)
500 g	16 oz (1 lb)
1 kg	32 oz (2 lb)

LIQUID MEASUREMENTS

Metric	Imperial
60 ml (¼ cup)	2 fl oz
75 ml (⅓ cup)	2½ fl oz
125 ml (½ cup)	4 fl oz
150 ml (⅔ cup)	5 fl oz (¼ pt)
175 ml (¾ cup)	6 fl oz
250 ml (1 cup)	8 fl oz
500 ml (2 cups)	16 fl oz
600 ml (2⅓ cups)	20 fl oz (1 pt)
1 litre (4 cups)	32 fl oz (1⅔ pt)

CONVERSIONS

Metric	Imperial
0.5 cm	¼ in
1 cm	½ in
2 cm	¾ in
2.5 cm	1 in
18 cm	7 in
20 cm	8 in

SPECIFIC MEASUREMENTS

1 cup flour	125 g	4 oz
1 cup cornflour	125 g	4 oz
1 cup sugar	250 g	8 oz
1 cup caster sugar	220 g	7 oz
1 cup brown sugar	185 g	6 oz
1 cup icing sugar	185 g	6 oz
1 cup butter	250 g	8 oz
1 cup honey	375 g	12 oz
1 cup fresh breadcrumbs	60 g	2 oz
1 cup dry breadcrumbs	125 g	4 oz
1 cup crushed biscuits	125 g	4 oz
1 cup dried fruits	185 g	6 oz
1 cup coconut, desiccated	90 g	3 oz
1 cup rolled oats	100 g	3½ oz
1 cup chopped nuts	125 g	4 oz
1 cup cocoa	125 g	4 oz

OVEN TEMPERATURES
Ovens do vary, so be guided by your own experience.

Temperatures	C Celsius	F Fahrenheit	Gas Mark
Very slow	120	250	1
Slow	150	300	2
Moderate	180	375	4
Hot	250	475	6

MICROWAVE
As most microwaves are different, cooking times will vary, so be guided by your manufacturer's advice. Our times are based on a 600w oven. Always under cook, test, and if necessary return to oven briefly.

ACKNOWLEDGEMENTS
The author wishes to acknowledge the following publications as sources of reference:
Australian Encyclopaedia (Grolier Society)
Australian Places (Reader's Digest).

INDEX

Main recipes are printed in bold type, food types are in italics, others are cross references.

A
Anzac Biscuits 57
Apple and Caraway Seed Bread with Cheese 35
Apple, Cradle Mountain 28
Asparagus, with walnut 41
Aussie Meat Pie with Tomato Sauce 42
B
Bananas in Chocolate Mud 22
Barramundi, black 66
Barramundi with Orange Sauce and Warm Salad 63
Barbecue prawns, in quandong chilli syrup 48
Beer batter, crocodile curry mayonnaise 64
Biscuits, Anzac 57
Black Barramundi 66
Blueberry Pie with Thick Lavender Cream 11
Boiled Fruit Cake 45
Bread and Butter Pudding 56
BREAD
Apple and Caraway Seed 35
Damper 60
Bread Roll Stuffed with Chicken Pâté 10
Buffalo fillet, seared with goat cheese 61
C
CAKES
Boiled Fruit Cake 45
Powder Puffs 23
Lamingtons 77
Carnival of Stir-fry Vegetables with Linguini Pasta 17
Cauliflower Cheese 9
Cheesy breadcrumbs 29
Chicken Kebabs in Peanut Sauce 70

Chicken pâté 10
Chickpea paste 51
Coulis, cucumber, capsicum 32
Crab, with coconut sauce 75
Cradle Mountain Apple 28
Crayfish Freshly Grilled with Lemon Butter 33
Crepe, potato 32
Crocodile in Beer Batter with Curry Mayonnaise 64
Croutons, garlic 26
Crumble, fruit 44
Custard, fig 39
D
Damper Dripping with Golden Syrup 60
Dilly Bag Steak Filled with Chickpea Paste 51
DRESSING
Coconut 75
Walnut 41
E
Eggs in a Hole 60
F
Fig custard 39
Flambe of Tropical Fruits 73
Fresh Asparagus Dressed with Walnut 41
Fruit cake, boiled 45
Fruit Crumble with Whipped Cream 44
G
Goat cheese balls 61
Green onion curls 70
I
Ice-cream, wattle seed 18
J
Jus mango 21
K
Kangaroo 'n Beer 38
Kebabs, chicken 70
L
Lamb in Macadamia Crust with Mango Jus 21
Lamb, roast 8

Lamingtons 77
Lavender cream 11
Lemon basket 16
Linguini pasta 17
M
Macadamia tuiles 18
Mango jus 21
MAYONNAISE
Avocado 20
Curry 64
MEAT
Buffalo fillet seared 61
Dilly bag steak 51
Kangaroo 'n beer 38
Lamb in macadamia crust 21
Lamb roast 8
Meat pie, Aussie 42
Oxtail stew 49
Pork ribs, stuffed 12
Mousse, pawpaw 67
Mousseline, tuna 52
Mud Crab with Coconut Sauce 75
Mussels Swimming in Garlic and Brandy 34
O
Our Own Pavlova 53
Oxtail Stew 49
Oysters, Sydney rock 16
P
Pasta, linguini 17
Pastry shell 20
Pâté, chicken 10
Pavlova 53
Pawpaw Mousse Wrapped in Spun Sugar 67
Peach Melba 13
Pear Poached in Red Wine with Fresh Fig Custard 39
PIE
Aussie Meat Pie 42
Blueberry 11
Pillows of Moreton Bay Bugs with Tomato Relish 71
Poached Tasmanian Trout with Lemon Almonds 27

Pork ribs, stuffed 12
Potato crepe 32
Potato nests 12
Potato Soup with Garlic Croutons 26
Powder Puffs 23
Prawns Barbecued in Quandong (or Apricot) Chilli Syrup 48
Pudding, bread and butter 56
Pumpkin Scones Smothered with Butter 74
Pumpkin Soup 74
Q
Quail with Olives and Sun-dried Tomato 40
Quandong syrup 48
R
Relish, tomato 71
Rice, saffron 70
Roast Lamb Dinner 8
Roast vegetables; onion, parsnip, potato, pumpkin, sweet potato
S
Salad, warm 63
SAUCE
Carnival, stir-fry vegetables 17
Cheese 9
Cherry 12
Chocolate mud 22
Coconut 75
Garlic and brandy 34
Melba 13
Mint 8
Orange 63
Peanut 70
Quandong (apricot) chilli syrup 48
Seafood 16
Scallops with Cheesy Topping 29
Scones, pumpkin 74
SEAFOOD
Barramundi; with orange sauce, 63
Black 66
Crayfish grilled, lemon butter 33
Moreton Bay bug pillows, tomato relish 71

Mud crab, coconut sauce 75
Mussels, garlic brandy 34
Oysters, seafood sauce 16
Prawns, barbecue with quandong syrup 48
Scallops with cheesy topping 29
Salmon smoked, potato crepes, capsicum, cucumber coulis 32
Snapper, whole with tuna mousseline 52
Trout poached, lemon almonds 27
Tuna mousseline, whole snapper 52
Smoked Salmon Wrapped in Potato Crepe with a Coulis Duet 32
SOUP
Potato 26
Pumpkin 74
Snapper, whole 52
Spun sugar 67
Stew, oxtail 49
Stock, fish 27
Stuffed Pork Ribs with Cherry Sauce 12
STUFFING
Chicken pâté 10
Pork ribs 12
Chickpea paste 51
Sydney Rock Oysters with a Lemon Basket 16
T
Tomato relish 71
Tropical fruits, flambe 73
Trout Poached in Fish Stock served with Lemon Almonds 27
Tuiles, macadamia 18
Tuna mousseline 52
W
Walnut dressing, asparagus 41
Wattle Seed Ice-cream with Macadamia Tuiles 18
Warm salad 63
Whole Snapper with Tuna Mousseline 52
Y
Yabbies in Green Coats 20

Australia Wide Cookbook

This edition published in 1995
by Ken Duncan Panographs® Pty Limited ACN 050 235 606
P.O. Box 15, Wamberal NSW 2260, Australia. Phone: (043) 676 777.

Copyright Photography:© Ken Duncan 1995
Copyright Text:© Valwyn McMonigal 1995

All rights reserved. No part of this publication may be reproduced, stored in a retrieval system, or transmitted in any form or by any means electronic, mechanical, photocopying, recording or otherwise without the prior written permission of the publisher.

Distributed in Australia by Peribo Pty Limited.
58 Beaumont Rd, Mt Kuringai. NSW. 2080. Phone: (02) 457 0011

Designer: Warren Penney
Food Stylist: Anne-Maree Kinley
Assistant: Julee Slater
Cover photography: Ken Duncan and Scott Papworth
Editor: Forsythe Editorial Services
Production: Victoria Jefferys

Colour separations by Litho Platemakers, Netley, S.A.
Printed In Hong Kong by South China Printing.

The National Library of Australia Cataloguing-in-Publication entry:

Duncan, Ken.
Australia wide cookbook.

Includes index.
ISBN 0 646 22694 0.

1. Cookery, Australian. 2. Australia - Pictorial works.
I. McMonigal, Valwyn. II. Title.

641.5994

Panographs® Pty Limited is a registered trademark of Ken Duncan
Australia Wide Holdings Pty Ltd.

Other titles in this series:
SPIRIT OF AUSTRALIA
SPECTACULAR SYDNEY
THE AUSTRALIA WIDE YEARBOOK
FROM FOREST TO SEA
BIRTH OF A NATION

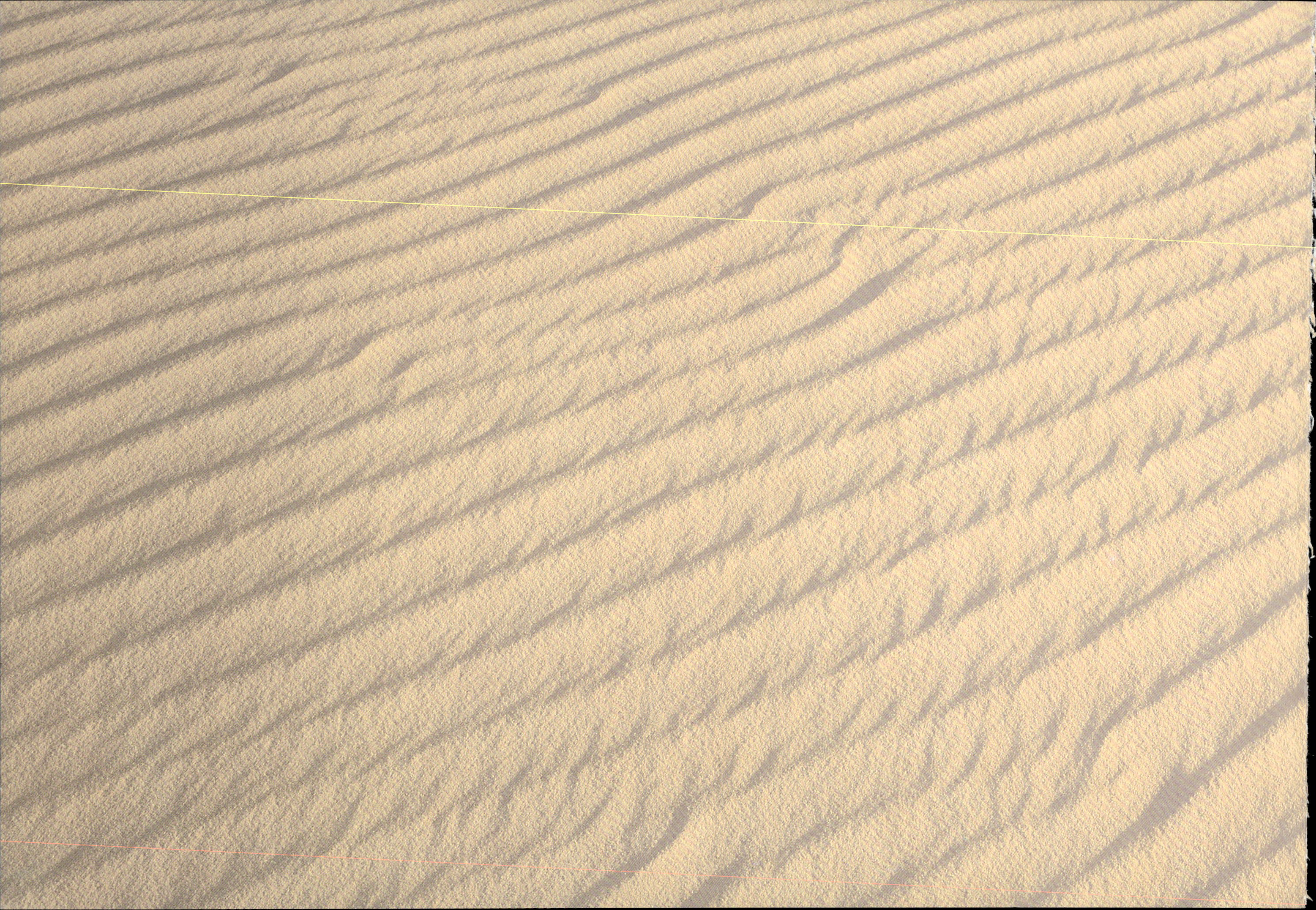